LOCAL AUTHOR DATE DUE

GAYLORD   PRINTED IN U.S.A.

Exciting Books From
WEBB RESEARCH GROUP, PUBLISHERS
→Availability and prices subject to change. This is a *partial* list←

The Lure of Medford - Documentary. Bert and Margie Webber. Popular look at Medford, how it started, uniquenesses. $12.95.

Jacksonville Oregon, Antique Town in a Modern Age – Documentary. Bert and Margie Webber. City is National Historic Landmark. $12.95.

Ashland – An Oregon Oasis; The Shakespeare Town. Janelle Davidson. Unique attractions in unusual town. $12.95.

Over the Applegate Trail to Oregon in 1946. Includes the Pringle Diary. Bert Webber. South approach of the Oregon Trail via Nevada's Black Rock Desert. How to get there. Astounding pictures! Pringle genealogy. $13.95

Oregon Covered Bridges – Expanded Edition; Bert and Margie Webber. (6 New Bridges!) Photos, how to find all 65 standing bridges. $10.95.

Ruch and the Upper Applegate Valley – Documentary. John and Marguerite Black. Ghost towns. Genealogically rich. $12.95

Single Track to Jacksonville; The Rogue River Valley Railway...– Documentary. Bert and Margie Webber. The 6-mile long railroad that connected Jacksonville to Medford. $12.95

Oregon's Great Train Holdup Bandits Murder 4 – Didn't Get A Dime! – Documentary. Bert and Margie Webber. Disaster in Siskiyou Mts with original pictures. $ 8.95.

This Is Logging & Sawmilling - Documentary - Helicopter logging, Railroad logging, Logging in snow, Fighting forest fires. Bert and Margie Webber. 247 amazing pictures, maps, etc. 160 pages. BIG BOOK ! 8½x11 $19.95.

Gold Mining in Oregon – Documentary; Includes How to Pan for Gold. Edited by Bert Webber. Data from Oregon State Dept. of Geology. All major gold mines located, how operated. 368 pages, pictures, maps – is "Mother Lode" book on Oregon gold mines! BIG BOOK ! 8½x11 $29.95.

Shipwrecks and Rescues on the Northwest Coast. Bert and Margie Webber Amazing true episodes of disasters $14.95.

Oregon's Seacoast Lighthouses (Includes nearby Shipwrecks). James A. Gibbs with Bert Webber Every Oregon coast lighthouse! $14.95.

Bayocean: The Oregon Town That Fell Into the Sea. Bert and Margie Webber. Includes Salishan, other erosion damages areas. $12.95.

Silent Siege-III: Japanese Attacks on North America in World War II; Ships Sunk, Air raids, Bombs Dropped, Civilians Killed. Bert Webber. Hundreds of Japanese attacks on 28 U.S. states – kids killed – and Canada never reported in papers due to agreement between gov't and press not to cause public panic. 304 pages, 462 photos, maps. BIG BOOK ! 8½x11 $28.95

"OUR BOOKS ARE HISTORICALLY ACCURATE AND FUN TO READ"
Shipping: Add $2.50 first book, 75¢ each extra book – except big *Silent Siege III , Gold Mining , Logging* shipping $5.95
Books Are Available Through All Independent Book Sellers
All Barnes & Noble Stores. Rush orders by Mail from Publisher
Send stamped, self-addressed envelope to speed copy of latest catalog to you.

WEBB RESEARCH GROUP, PUBLISHERS
P.O. Box 314 Medford, OR 97501 USA

PLAZA – ASHLAND – JANUARY 1, 1997 Photo courtesy of Gloria Fowler

American Red Cross Emergency Relief Vehicle brings lunches to Nauvoo trailer court during cleanup a week after the flood.

FLOOD!

Ashland Devastated – New Year's Day 1997
—An Oregon Documentary—
Bert and Margie Webber LOCAL AUTHOR

PLAZA – ASHLAND – JANUARY 1, 1997   Photo courtesy of Gloria Fowler

Webb Research Group Publishers
Books About the Oregon Country

Copyright © Bert Webber 1997
All Rights Reserved
Under Berne International Copyright Convention
Printed in Oregon U.S.A.

Please direct all inquiries to the publisher:
Published by
WEBB RESEARCH GROUP PUBLISHERS
Books About the Oregon Country
P. O. Box 314
Medford, Oregon 97501

About the 160 Photographs

Cover Pictures: (Front) Courtesy of Joe Frodsham, Medford
                 (Back)   Courtesy of Bert Webber, Central Point

Credit for each photograph appears with the picture except for the covers which are credited here, and photographs made by the authors, which are not credited unless they appear within a group of pictures made by others on the same page.

Library of Congress Cataloging-in-Publication Data:

Webber, Bert
  FLOOD! : Ashland Devastated – New Year's Day, 1997 : an Oregon Documentary / Bert and Margie Webber.
    p.   cm.
  Includes bibliographical references and index.
  ISBN 0-936738-02-2
  1. Floods –Oregon–Ashland–History–20th century. 2. Ashland (Or.)–History. I. Webber, Margie. II. Title.
  F884.A6W48   1997   97-252
  979.5'27–dc21   CIP

Contents

Introduction	15
Roving Cameraman-Reporter Covers a Flood	19
Report of Damage Caused by Roca Creek	50
TV Cameraman Swims for his Life, Rescues Woman	51
Calle Guanajuato (Guanajuato Way) Hit Hard	52
Disaster Services	
American Red Cross –Chartered by Congress	59
The Salvation Army – Always Ready	65
Street Corner Toileting; It's Still a Privy Even if It's Made of Yellow Plastic	72
Hospital Safe – Is On High Ground	73
Emigrant Lake Dam and the Talent Irrigation District	78
Mobile Homes – Trailers No Match for Flood	80
Rogue River Gorge Choked For Decades....	94
Flood Control - U. S. Army Corps of Engineers	95
Earlier Floods	97
High Water in Central Point; Griffin Creek on a Rampage	103
Some Other Areas Troubled by Flood	119
Covering the New Year's Day 1997 Flood; Newspapers and Television	133
Appendix	
The Red Cross	137
The Salvation Army	139
About the Authors	141
Bibliography and Reading List	142
Index	146

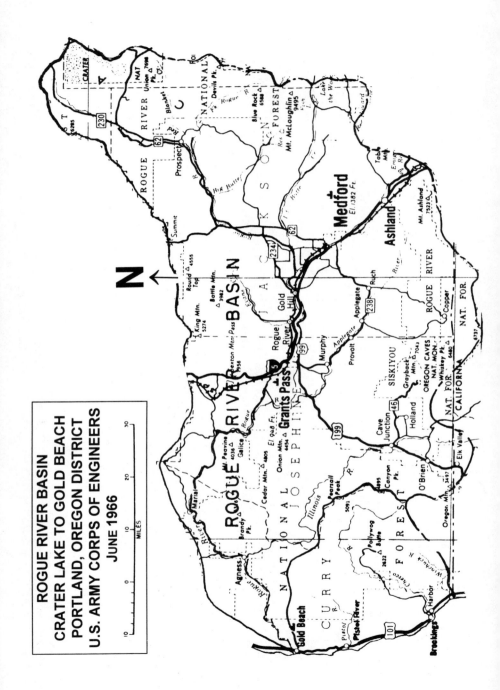

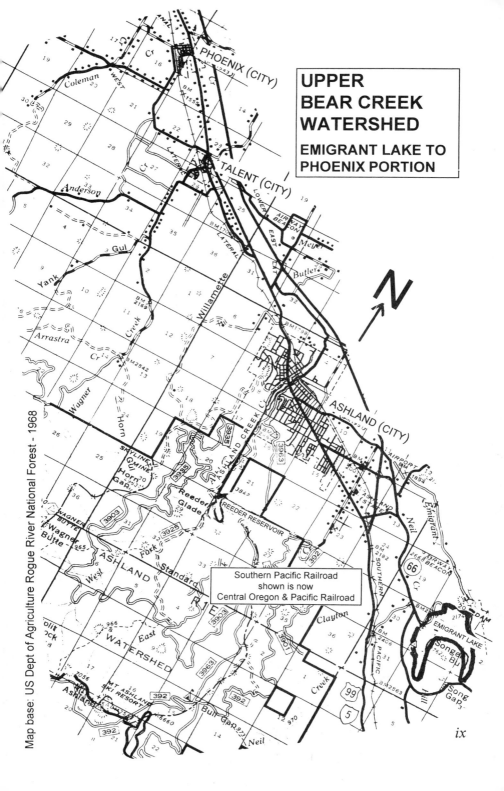

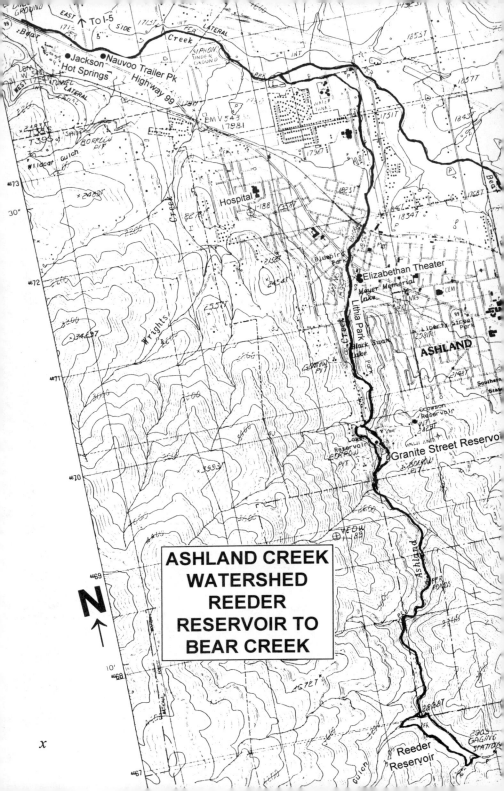

Remains of north end of Lithia Park and washed-out Winburn Way and Calle Guanajuato
—Courtesy of Joe Frodsham

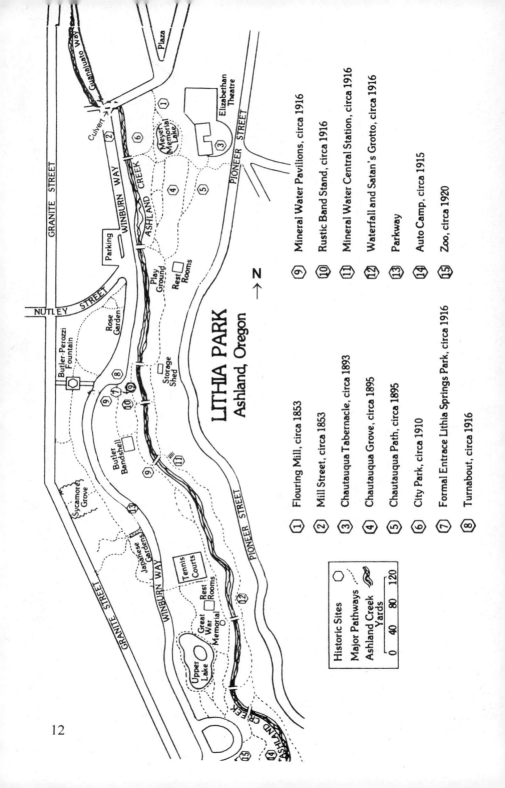

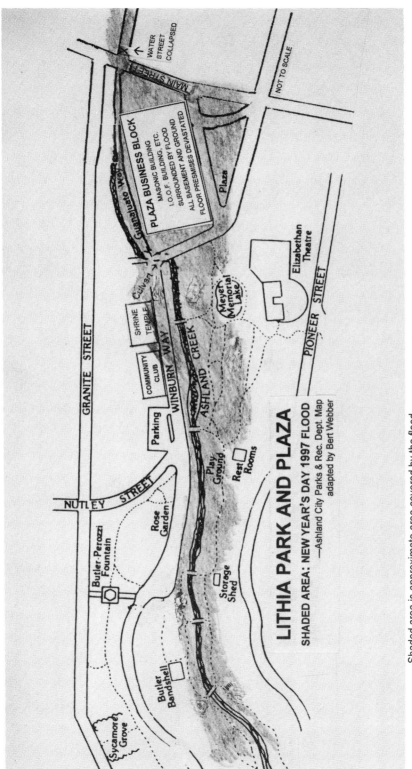

Shaded area is approximate area covered by the flood.

Ashland Plaza businesses were surrounded by flood January 1, 1997
—Courtesy of Joe Frodsham

Introduction

A rainy weather forecast by the National Weather Service had been repeated for several days therefore many New Year's Eve revelers had to change plans to accommodate the weather.

Rain seemed to be falling all over Oregon and in many places with vigor. To name a couple, Johnson Creek, an often wildly-flowing stream whenever there is heavy rain, in Multnomah County (Portland), went over its banks. The Tualatin River, Washington and Clackamas Counties, normally twisting, sluggish and often muddy, whipped itself into a frenzy and took shortcuts across land between its usual sharp curves. At the canal that connects with the Tualatin that feeds Oswego Lake, the lake, the centerpiece for the city of Lake Oswego, the water was out of its banks.

In Southern Oregon, when Ashland Creek started to spill over its banks in Lithia Park and at Winburn Way, there did not seem to be much initial worry. It had happened before. Some claim that Ashland Creek caused havoc as far back as 1888. The creek rose in 1964 (an event many folks remember) – a bad flood a week before Christmas (a sad experience for those with property near it)*, then again in 1974. There was some high water in the 1980's. In late December of 1996, Ashland Creek was on the prowl but fell back.

Rain continued and the water in the rain gauge at the weather office at the Rogue Valley International – Medford Airport, fifteen miles to the north, started to climb.

Early on January 1, the new year was greeted with a steady increase in rain – it measured 3.5 inches in 24 hours. As a result, all creeks and rivers rose some approaching flood stage, others surpassing that measurement.

New Year's revelers at the Plaza, Ashland's famed historical area, and shop owners there took notice. The National Weather Service had put out warning and the creek, now swiftly flowing, could no longer be contained within its banks. The heavy rainfall bloated hills which gave away as mud slides. A sea of mud, along with crashing trees, during the dense rain storm flooded against homes on Granite Street causing three of them

---

* Refer to bibliography

to slide a distance down the hill.

"Hill"? Ashland, 1,951 feet elevation, is in the foothills of the Siskiyou Mountains with Mt. Ashland, 7,533 feet elevation, only eight straight-line miles to the south. The descent of the creek from Reeder Reservoir, Ashland's water supply within the mountains does not slow down when it "hits" town but continues its flow until it joins with Bear Creek near the town's northern limits.

On January 1, 1997, Bear Creek was already full and was causing some concern to the southeast of town.* When Ashland Creek's deluge crashed into Bear Creek, the combined water roared downstream through the Nauvoo Trailer Park where the power of the water threw automobiles, trailers, motor homes, and trees in every direction. The trailer park was hastily evacuated in the nick of time. No lives were lost and no one was seriously hurt.

Within hours, emergency services moved into Ashland. Warnings went out over radio and television that the sewage treatment plant was overwhelmed with an exhortation that flushing toilets could cause raw sewage to flow into the already flooded streets. Then came the announcement that the fresh water supply, for the city's 18,000 people, had been shut down. The town's paper, the Ashland *Daily Tidings* headlined:

> DON'T DRINK THE WATER – MASSIVE FLOODING FORCES SHUTDOWN OF ASHLAND'S WATER SYSTEM, POSSIBLY FOR AS LONG AS TWO WEEKS.

Emergency contracts went out by telephone for portable toilets to be perched around town. Then the National Guard arrived with huge flatbed trucks carrying drinking water in 3,000 gallon bladders, and some smaller tankers. Plastic bottle manufacturers in Portland, 300 miles away, donated thousands of gallon size jugs for the people to pick up, fill with drinking water (that came from Medford 12 miles to the north) and carry home.

The American Red Cross Emergency Services mobilized its forces and sent trucks, with two of them coming from Kansas. The vans arrived with ready-to-eat food as some school gyms as

---

* See chapter "Emigrant Lake and Dam."

Three of the local newspapers that covered the flood. (TOP) *Ashland Daily Tidings* (CENTER) Medford *Mail Tribune* (LOWER) *Central Valley Times*. An extensive list of articles about the flood appears in the bibliography of this book starting on page 142.

well as the National Guard Armory in Medford became emergency shelters. And in the middle of the stress, a new baby was born in Ashland Community Hospital.

> **A tip of the Webbers' hats to Ashland city officials.**
> **From the mayor (Ms. Cathy Golden) along the line to mud-mucking heavy equipment operators who were 1) Honest and forthright with answers to questions; 2) The keen ability of employees to work together with no interdepartmental friction; 3) Demonstrated ability to listen to public inquiry and to make tactical decisions for the good of the city and of its citizens without bureaucratic delays.**

And so it was: Happy (?) New Year in Ashland, Oregon.

—0—

Many people cooperated with us in providing interviews, photographs, and special help so this book could be put together. Of great importance is to mention that while the Ashland Plaza area was considered dangerous and was protected by police lines, the Ashland Police Department, which set up a street corner information stand, escorted store owners, their workers and qualified visitors into the restricted areas. On two occasions, we were provided with police escorts to make many of the pictures appearing in this book.

Of course there were many more folks we could have talked with, and many more pictures we could have included. But a book must stop at an editorially determined place otherwise it would become so think no one could afford to buy a copy.

We wish to thank the professional reference librarians and the volunteers who work in the Reference Department at the Jackson County Library for their help in documenting a number of historical matters included here.

Comments about this book and the flood of New year's Day 1997 can be sent to us in care of the publisher whose address is on page *vi*, but it may be that every letter cannot be personally acknowledged.

Bert and Margie Webber
Central Point, Oregon
February 14, 1997

Roving Cameraman-Reporter
What He Learned

As I traveled through the damaged areas making pictures and talking with people, I was seized with my observation that a good news-person, that is, one who has a real "nose for news," could be looking at a different subject, each a potential feature story, at the rate of about one-a-minute. No news agency could ever cover them all. On six different days I said to myself that I had enough pictures but each day as I was preparing to go home, I found myself reloading a camera for more, and more and more pictures. Will the subjects ever stop?

How nice it is to live at a safe distance from the flood where one gets a good night's sleep, awakes to the perc of a coffee pot, a heated and buttered "Danish, and one can enjoy a refreshing morning shower before going to work.

What of the flooded areas? Think about it:

Marie, her husband Archie, 9-year old Gretchen and 15-year old Susan had been summoned from their beds about midnight with a banging on their mobile home door and the shout of a volunteer, "Leave now, the water is rising."

Some managed to grab a few things, sometimes little more than clothing to cover their backs, then stumble through cold, foot-deep flooding Bear Creek to higher ground. With a distant flash, all the lights went out. Then stand and peer into the night as the waters rose to the doorstep, then into their home eventually to a depth of over four feet. There was no morning shower, no hot coffee and nowhere to immediately go. As dawn broke, the sight became devastating. The creek was no longer its picturesque gurgling eight-foot wide stream but was now over one hundred feet wide of crashing muddy water carrying trees, automobiles, parts of buildings and anything that was in its way.

A geology teacher said that Bear Creek didn't like the man-made route in which it flowed, that the creek had its own mind and went its own way.

(TOP) **Ashland Police Dept. set up a street-corner Information desk at the edge of the Plaza.** (CENTER) **Volunteer sign-up table on a below-freezing morning.** (INSET) **Someone loaned a kerosene heater.** (LOWER) **Most restaurants were closed due to no fresh water, but those open advertised the fact with window signs.**

There was plenty of work needing doing and over 900 volunteers signed up during a period of about two weeks.
(LOWER) **Tessah, 9, and her mother, Linda Joseph, were among the volunteers. One of the many tasks: shovel mud!**

Joe Frodsham flew over Ash' the worst of the storm abated a some of which he loaned, for which cluded here.

R. Loren and Gloria Fowler mad through the crowd of curious onlookers Creek as its high tide of crashing flood w into some businesses on the Plaza. Each pro photos for our use here. We thank them.

On New Year's Day, as the rain continu Ashland Creek scurried through the Plaza with abating, onlookers, many with video cameras, crov camera perch in town to record the view. This was over the creek on C Street which presented a full vi waters rushing through the Plaza and into the 20-foot d hole that had earlier been Water Street. The Ashland announced that the biggest obstacle to emergency relief e1 was the extra traffic and spectators. In short order, access i Ashland from the north, primarily from Interstate-5 was close to all traffic.

Because of a serious mud slide in California, near Dunsmuir, 75 miles south of Ashland, Interstate-5 was closed to traffic at Ashland. Most motels were open and filled rapidly but offered no drinking water, no showers and no toilets. On learning these factors, some motorists back-tracked to motels in Medford.

Hundreds of volunteers signed the register at Ashland City Hall then went to be of help wherever required. The first urgency appeared to be need for people to fill sand bags then distribute the filled bags in low-lying areas. Working with full bags of sand is not easy. To be effective, the bags need to be fairly heavy as the force of the flood striking the bags can dislodge them. A well-filled bag of dry sand weighs between 40 and 50 pounds. Efforts to pass full bags by the "chain-gang" method often fail as many volunteers do not have the stamina for handling such weights for more than a few minutes at a time. At some sand bag filling locations, volunteers organized themselves into "rotating" crews to keep the work going.

Bear Creek roared through the Nauvoo Trailer Park north of

Ashland then flooded Highway 99 to nearly drown Jackson Hot Springs trailer village. Firemen from Fire District No. 5 turned out to rescue many dozens of people whose trailers had been flooded.

(Of the approximately 6,000 trailers in Oregon, the largest number are in Jackson County. Of these, an estimated 20 percent – 1,200 – were a total loss or were damaged.)

The rain-soaked hills of Ashland started to give way sending mud sloshing downward. Above Granite Street, the mud caught several homes and wrecked them.

All of the center of Lithia Park, where the creek runs, and the lower end of the park, was inundated as the creek changed course by running over the top of its plugged culvert at Winburn Way and spilling into the Plaza. It also drowned short Guanajuata Way, and its businesses. The narrow way runs behind the Plaza business houses.

The city declared all of Lithia Park "off limits." Access to Hillah Shrine Temple and Ashland Community Club was cut because of the inundation of Winburn Way which for a length, became the raging "Winburn River."

Writing in the *Ashland Daily Tidings* on January 2, 1997, Managing editor Jeff Keating noted:

> The top draw in Ashland New year's Day was the Plaza, but not for the usual reasons. Shopping, sight-seeing and people-watching were the last things on spectators' minds as they watched flood waters race down sidewalks, and saw Ashland Creek surge over its banks and wreak havoc throughout downtown. ... Grab your snorkles, flippers and wet-suits and make like a duck. Enjoy life in the Pacific Northwest – at least the parts that aren't under water.

How can a restaurant operate without running water? Because dish washing machines had to be shut off due to the lack of water, a number of restaurants went right ahead with business using paper plates and disposable plastic utensils. For kitchen-use water, they hauled in gallons from the National Guard trucks, or set up mini-water systems from large borrowed or leased tanks. Because hand-washing may be limited, cooks and

> **Does your coffee taste different this morning? Where did you get the water?**

Remains of north end of Lithia Park and washed-out Winburn Way; proximity with Shakespeare Theaters
—Courtesy of Joe Frodsham

> **"Water, Water, Everywhere**
> **Nor Any Drop to Drink"**
> —Rhyme of the Ancient Mariner. Pt. II. Stanza 9
> Samuel Taylor Colridge 1772-1834
>
> It didn't matter what club or activity or school one planned to attend during the first few days of January in Ashland or Talent, one's plans were altered or in reality, cancelled.
>
> Schools, set to start the new year right after the holiday did not unlock their doors. There was no drinking water. No water to prepare cafeteria lunches. No fresh water to add to the class-room fish tank. No water to flush toilets and no water for the showers in the athletic departments.
>
> No water — period.

food handlers wore rubber gloves. Although renting tanker systems, which provide somewhat less than usual pressure, is expensive, it is a means for keeping restaurants open.

Ashland was flooded not only by several creeks that went out-of-bounds, but flooded with travelers who were stuck in town due to the closure of the freeway (I-5) by mud slides. People needed meal services and employees needed to work even if part of the city was shut down due to the emergency.

Gerry Lehrburger, a co-owner with Barbara McKie at Jackson Hot Springs, was pretty sober about the damage to his property. Automobiles that could not be moved in time were strewn around the property, fences were down, trees uprooted, RV's and trailers parked there sustained major damage from rapidly rising Bear Creek water.

A resident, lucky to have a canoe, used it to rescue people who became stranded. One renter, who was a writer, said he lost his computer in which he said there was 16-years worth of work. The writer, Ben Morgan, quipped that he did not lose his car, a Trans-Am, because it was away from the premises in a repair shop.

As the water drained from the park, thick "gumbo" (mud) remained to a depth that high-center 4-wheel drive vehicles were all that were recommended to drive the grounds.

Dick Finnell, who plays trombone in the Swing Kings Big Band, was on the way to his Phoenix address after a New Year's

Eve gig. He saw flood waters ahead on the road, and was proceeding gingerly when his engine quit. With his car stopped, he

> ### All 4-Wheels – Mired
>
> "So I own a new compact car with all-wheel drive. I was quick to find out that just because all the wheels are drivers, my little light car was no match for even five inches of mud. I was up to about 8 miles an hour and managed to get stuck about 20 to 30 feet into the mire. All my car did was spin wheels and throw mud. My friend with a Bronco, who was nearby, saw my problem so drove up and gently pushed me out."

had to force the door open because of the water pressure against it. On opening his door, water flooded in to his seated waist then he crawled out. Other cars, on the submerged road were splashing along causing waves in the flood. Although dressed in his Tuxedo, he worked his way around to the front of th car and pushed his car nearly 100 feet to safety.

By this time a neighbor drove up with Finnell's wife, and got a ride home. Later, in the American Red Cross Emergency Shelter. He recalled:

That night was something to remember. I was soaked, freezing cold, and tired from pushing the car through the flood. The first thing I did was go home, change into some dry clothing, then at the shelter we were assigned to cots. But there wasn't any sleep due to the almost constant noise of workers setting up cots the rest of the night.

Finnell reported it cost 1,200 bucks to get his car fixed.

> ### Boy Scout's Volunteer
>
> In Talent, a Boy Scout troop turned out to help. One of its duties was at water trucks where they assisted the public by filling jugs. Officials said there would be plenty of water if people would limit themselves to 5 gallons per person a day.
> Other Boy Scouts helped with serving meals at Talent Community Hall to about 50 refugees who stayed there Tuesday night.

Dr. Robert "Chip" Zundel, a dentist, occupies an attractive brick office building near the freeway, Luman Road and Bear

(TOP) With no warnings yet posted, several drivers were caught in their cars when the vehicles quit in high water after dark on Luman Road, Phoenix. (LOWER) Flooded flatland between Bear Creek and Dr. Zundel's dental office, created "Zundel Lake."
—Courtesy: Laura and Dr. Robert Zundel

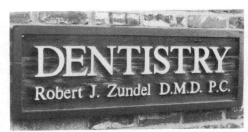

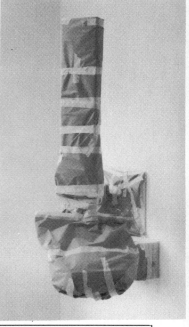

"Zundel Lake" surrounded and flooded the office, therefore the dentist and his staff moved and stored equipment and other furnishings into rented van. Contractor cloaked a wall-mounted x-ray unit in paper in preparation for refinishing the walls and floors. (LOWER). **New dental chairs,** (FACING PAGE), **about $4,000 each, were required.**

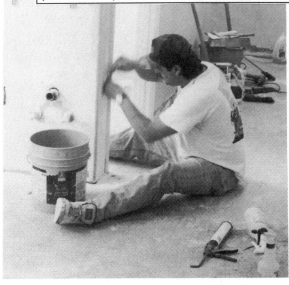

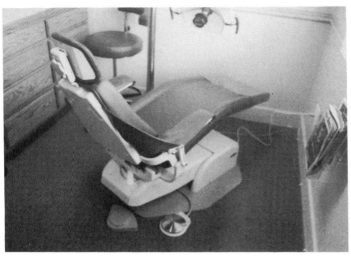

Creek on the east edge of Phoenix. The creek overflowed its banks and spread across the lowland flooding Zundel's building. When he was able to make his way to his office, he found the place caked in almost six inches of sticky mud. The flood water "fried" the electric works in his dental chairs which rendered all the chairs a total loss.

He rented a large van and had it parked next to his building. Then he stripped the office of furniture and apparatus, placing everything inside the van for storage while contractors totally refinished his dental office. In the meantime, his receptionist took the appointment book to her home where she spent many hours and days with her telephone rescheduling patients. Dr. Zundel was forced by the flood to shut down for nearly three weeks, sadly realizing that the damage to his premises, equipment and loss of business was well above $50,000.

Sharon James, who lives in the hills out of Talent, reported her situation:

> The flood broke the county road in six places and it was 'iffy' if our 4-wheel drive would get us out. So we, and a friend from Eagle Point, stayed put. We watched movies on TV, baked a lot of goodies then ate a lot of goodies for two days. I lost one day's work because of the road.

Virginia Westerfield lives on one of Ashland's city streets which is on the side of a hill. When there is heavy rain, and because of some springs higher on the hill, seepage gets into her basement and often leaves a puddle on floor. In the present instance, the heavy rain and the springs put a foot of water in her

THE FLOOD — "PHOTO-OP" OF THE SEASON

The flood turned out to be a huge "photo-op."

It appears that just about everyone who could shot pictures of the flood and its aftermath did so. Kathy Fowler, photo-lab supervisor and work-flow coordinator at Frodsham's main photo finishing plant in Medford, told us that as the weather cleared and cameras came out, their daily number of rolls of film processed in their Ashland store and in the Medford main plant more than doubled.

In Ashland, the plant was closed one day, the New Year's Day holiday. This provided an opportunity for Jack Fowler, equipment maintenance manager, to make a seasonal overhaul of the printers. But for the next several days, due to the Ashland Water Department being shut down, Rod Fowler, Ashland manager, and Jason Hill, an employee, made two trips a day hauling water from the Medford shop in 5-gallon jugs, 12 at a time, to keep the plant operating.

In Medford, extra workers were brought in. Kathy, and senior photo-lab technicians Dulcie McDowell, Marne Astell, Leanna Dritchas, Rachelle Milner, Shelly Jorstad, and junior techs Steven Pope and Kari Ellison, put in overtime hours trying to keep up with demand. "For a few days, our usual 1-hour service schedule went out the window," quipped Kathy recalling how the crew fed film rolls (including ours) into processing tanks and hovered over printing machines for many hours.

Customer service personnel Jackie Thompson, Mike Niles and Hazel Frodsham, and three part-time extras, set up additional counter areas to accommodate camera-toters who patiently waited in double lines that extended to the door.

basement which included soaking the lower part of a more than 50-years old big, heavy piano. She was able to use a garden hose to siphon most of the water out of the basement. Days later, when the basement held considerably less water, she found a card-board box of keep-sake cards and letters from former students, which became soaked and soggy in the flood. (She taught band at Rogue River High School many years ago.) Virginia flattened the letters carefully and left them on kitchen tables to dry, which they did.

The majority of Ashland's people went along with the interruptions of daily living and accepted many make-shift measures to keep their town running. But there were exceptions. The National Guard went to great expense (tax dollars at work) in supplying heavy trucks, tankers, and servicing personnel on what was called the "Fresh Water Detail." But some persons could not abide by emergency procedures. As an example: Wendy's Old Fashioned Hamburger restaurant arranged to have a 2,500 gallon water tank installed on its lot so they could stay open for business. At closing time on a certain night, the manager determined there was close to 1,800 gallons in the tank, but on his arrival the next morning, he discovered that presumably thirsty people had tapped his tank for 1,200 gallons leaving only about 600 gallons on which to start the day's business. Wendy's was alarmed to note that this was the second theft of large amounts of water during the crisis.

Hundreds of people were forced to evacuate their homes when flood waters, and accompanying mud or sand, invaded their residences. At the Ashlander Apartments, eighteen units on the ground floor became local "disaster areas" as a result of the flooding of Hamilton Creek which, while rampaging, broke a main-line water pipe. The creek, mixed with drinking water from the broken pipe, swished down the hill, went through the apartment complex as well as blocking Clay Street and Siskiyou Blvd. The residents were moved by the management to other properties. In the aftermath of drying, some of those apartments looked like housekeeping had been going on in a giant sand box as there was up to three feet of sand in the buildings.

The amount of seepage into the Shrine's Hillah Temple had been kept to a minimum because of two factors: 1) The building was on the periphery of the flood and the totally inundated Winburn Way which is next to the Plaza, 2) Tightly fitted doors. Seeping flood waters threatened the carpet but apparently did little damage. Of concern was the status of several boxes of music, stored on the floor used by the Shrine Band and Southern Oregon Concert Band, which rehearse in the temple. Luckily, the seepage did not reach the music. But the 70-member concert band temporarily lost its rehearsal hall.

> The Mount Ashland Ski area had been open a short while when its scheduled operations were abruptly changed. Rain melted a lot of the snow base and caused dangerous road conditions including a slide on the access road.

Mud slide descended upon homes on Granite Street, wrecking some and leaving the street full of mud (LOWER) **Carrier from *Ashland Daily Tidings* wades through the mud to deliver paper.**

    The routine schedule of incoming freight trucks of grocery re-stock items for the supermarkets was interrupted early-on. When Ashland's potable water supply was shut off, Safeway Stores placed an urgent order for 1-gallon containers of drinking water. The next truck to arrive set off 20 pallets of jugged water – about 4,000 gallons. Then the driver drove the truck to Ashland Community Hospital where an additional 4,000 gallons had been ordered. With some schedule interruptions, the hospital continued to operate.*

---

* See chapter "Hospital Safe – Is On High Ground

Ashland Creek, normally under Winburn Way in a culvert, flooded across Winburn Way as the creek, assisted by heavy equipment, carved a new channel. Hillah Shrine Temple was largely spared by mere inches.
(LOWER) Businesses on the Plaza side of Winburn Way were not as lucky. Sand was hauled from Renaissance Rose shop by many wheelbarrow loads.

The newspapers and television stations pleaded with people not to get in the way of workers, especially in the early days of the flood when water was still cascading through the Plaza. But the message the people got seems to have been to "stay out of downtown" instead of just "stay out of the damaged Plaza area." According to numerous merchants interviewed in the week of

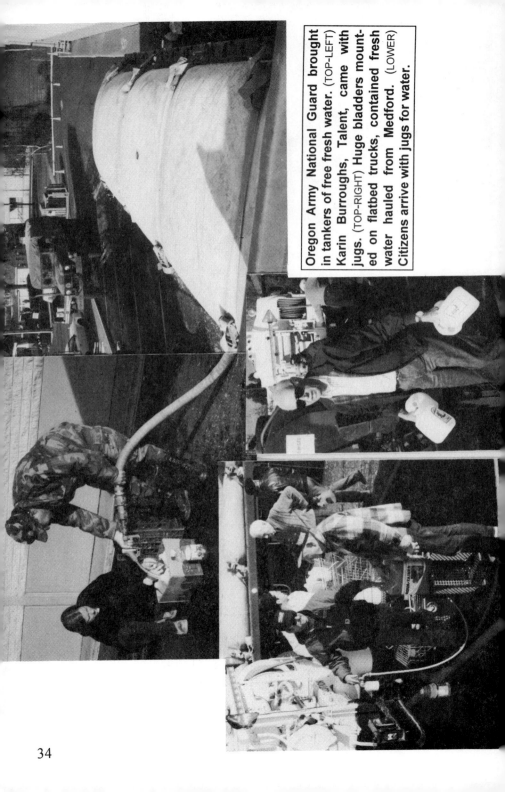

Oregon Army National Guard brought in tankers of free fresh water. (TOP-LEFT) Karin Burroughs, Talent, came with jugs. (TOP-RIGHT) Huge bladders mounted on flatbed trucks, contained fresh water hauled from Medford. (LOWER) Citizens arrive with jugs for water.

(TOP) Commercial vendors rushed to deliver drinking water to those who did not want to go to into town for the free water. (LOWER) A gentleman, who pleaded not to be identified, permitted neighbors to dip all the "clean and chlorinated" water they needed from his pool.

January 13th – two weeks after the start of the flood – none of the media ever made a correction saying just to stay away from the "Plaza." Thus, as reported to the writer, business was been slow, very slow – slower that a usual January because, merchants related, the scary pictures of conditions in the Plaza were believed to be the same conditions throughout the downtown area. The vast majority of Ashland businesses was never hurt by flood waters as most of the town's business district is at a much higher elevation than the Plaza.

Bloomsbury Books, on East Main Street, as an example, was closed for the national holiday, New Year's Day, but reopened on January 2 as did most businesses that were not hit by flood waters. A book shop staff person said, "We brought our own drinking water in bottles from home and used the chemical toilets across the street." Several merchants said that business has been very slow in getting re-started.

Fire Departments in every city, town and rural area engage in extensive homework on a continuing basis to know the access ways to reach every part of their districts. They often practice, especially in training sessions, with alternate routes to get into parts of towns when certain streets are blocked. Plan "A" might be the answering of a call on the usual city streets and roads. Plan "B," "C", and so on would be the alternate routes to get to the same ultimate location. Regardless of which streets might be blocked by the flood, Ashland's Fire Department had its alternate routes well planned.

Persons affected by the flood were offered relief from a number of sources. The Internal Revenue Service said that certain reports due January 15, could be delayed a week. But in reality, many flood victims were just as bad off a week later as they had been earlier.

Various banks announced policies of working with refugees from the flood who needed emergency loans for their damaged businesses. There would be no setup fees, filing fees and faster-than-usual processing time as well as increased credit limits to present customers was promised. One bank set up emergency loan procedures while donating $50,000 to the American Red Cross disaster program. It also waived late fees for loan cus-

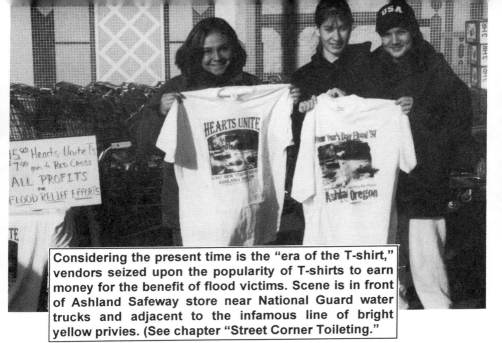

Considering the present time is the "era of the T-shirt," vendors seized upon the popularity of T-shirts to earn money for the benefit of flood victims. Scene is in front of Ashland Safeway store near National Guard water trucks and adjacent to the infamous line of bright yellow privies. (See chapter "Street Corner Toileting.")

tomers.*

Two independent T-shirt producers created special designs, produced T-shirts and put up card table sales outlets at supermarket doors and other locations from Ashland to Central Point. The proceeds from sales went to American Red Cross Disaster Relief and to a special account at a local bank for uninsured, displaced refuges from the flood.

At Talent, a few miles from Ashland, the city gets most of its water from its pump house on the edge of Bear Creek. Early in the flood, the creek's water undermined the concrete block pump house, tipped the building to a dangerous angle and flooded the equipment with muddy water effectively shutting off 60 percent of the city's water supply. One of the reasons for advertising on the television news programs about the city's loss of the Bear Creek water system, was that while water remained

---

* This was Bank of America which has a tradition of helping customers when the chips are down. In 1906, in the days immediately after the disastrous San Francisco earthquake and fire, while other bankers went home to lick their wounds, A. P. Gianninni, the founder of what became the Bank of America, set up a card table on Montgomery Street outside his ruined bank and opened for business personally making emergency cash loans on the spot. His vaults burned out, he kept the bank's money in a lettuce crate in the back of his buckboard. —(*Biography of a Bank*)

Talent's pump house tilted, fell into Bear Creek effectively shutting off fresh water to Talent.

in the town's tank, the authorities pleaded that it not be used for domestic purposes as the Fire Department might need it in case of a bad fire. The National Guard set up its water trucks in Talent as it did in Ashland, and chemical portable toilets appeared in town. Talent has an older pumping station on the other side of town that draws from Wagner Creek. Wagner Creek also went out of its banks and that system (40 percent of the city's supply) also went off-line. But the Wagner Creek pump was overhauled and went back to work within a few days with warnings to the people not to overuse it. The pumping station on Bear Creek is to be righted and mounted on skids (with a new pump) therefore the small building can be pulled away from the creek with a tractor in future high-water situations.

Schools in Ashland and Talent, including Southern Oregon State College, postponed the usual day-after-New Year's Day reopening due to the flood. In Talent, which was unable to get its fresh water system working up to speed for weeks, when schools opened there, physical education classes went on as usual but there were no showers. And users of the "facilities," were directed to use "it" several times before flushing. Drinking water and hand-washing sites were set up but the school lunch program underwent a severe change in menus, which were served on paper plates, because of limited water and no use of the dishwashers.

The New Year's Day 1997 Flood forced hundreds of workers out of jobs as their places of employment "went under" due to flood damage or lack of water. The Oregon State Employment

> ## **Flooded Out of Home or Business Can be Stressful**
> ## **A Check-List**
> - Be patient. Things will work out.
> - Be very glad if you have money in a bank and the money is readily available as you will need it.
> - If one has insurance, keep alert as claims people sometimes seem to take forever and may not represent your loss(es) in the manner one might expect. Have a lawyer handy.
> - Use a pair of gloves and waterproof boots if you must physically move heavy, dirty objects.
> - Make every effort to keep your feet dry.
> - Pray for sunshine and for a light breeze as sunshine is good for the soul and with the wind will help dry things.
> - Volunteers who were not directly affected by a flood move in with mops, buckets, shovels, wet-dry vacuums, wheel barrows, chain saws, axes, pickup trucks, ready-to-eat food, the "staff of life: hot coffee"! Bring a case of pint-size bottles of drinking water – soda pop.
> - Plan on many weeks, even months, to get back your balance for daily living and work.
> - Maintain a sense of humor.
> - Why pray when you can worry?
> - Thank God for your situation as it might have been worse.
> - Get up. Get Going, The next time might be worse.

Department extended its hours to include Saturdays as the now unemployed came in to file claims.

The "went under" included those businesses with physical loss of premises because of the flood, as well as businesses that had to close because of no fresh water. These included primarily restaurants, motels and schools.

Rescue workers observed that many of the people they assisted from flooded living quarters had pets with them. Veterinarians said they had not discovered any serious injury to pets and admonished owners to serve bottled water to their animals and not let pets drink contaminated water.

> Ashland city authorities said that the damage to buildings on the Plaza and in the first block of Winburn Way, due to having been undermined by the flood, or the flood depositing so much mud on some floors that it overburdened the floors, was very severe in 1997 but that the streets sustained more damage in 1974.

(TOP) **Jackson Hot Springs under water New Year's Day. Note half-submerged telephone booths (arrow).**
—Courtesy: Michael E. Webber. (LOWER) **Six days later, the once attractive lawn was a mess of mud as much as six inches thick in places.**
—author photo

> Numerous restaurants bought advertising space in the newspapers announcing they were
>
> **OPEN FOR BUSINESS – WATER NOT CONTAMINATED**
>
> Some had always operated on tested and approved well water while others, on city water, had arranged for temporary storage tanks to be installed at their places then had the tanks plumbed into the shops' systems.

Three people were rescued by a sheriff's deputy when the officer saw a light beam from a flashlight. Zoeann and Calvin Ross and Terry Coffee were in their home next to Jackson Hot Springs when Bear Creek waters seeped over Highway 99 then filled the low area south of the road where both properties are located. The officer had been directed to look at conditions, and for people at the Hot Springs and spotted the light on his way there. With a borrowed boat, he managed to work his way under the carport's roof to pick up the people who were in swirling neck-deep water. These folks lost everything as the water rose to the height of the house's roof. The Rosses said they had survived floods at this property in earlier years but the New Year's Day 1997 flood would be their last as they would not rebuild on the property. At the Hot Springs, two mobile homes, five vehicles and a boat were the casualties.

At the Ashlander Apartments, at 2234 Siskiyou Blvd, a mile southwest from the flooded Plaza, havoc was caused when water from Hamilton Creek over-ran its banks and cascaded into the lower floor of the complex. Ordinarily, the creek is "a cute little creek that trickles by our door," said a receptionist at the complex. Of the 178 apartments, 18 were destroyed and 32 evacuated with an estimated loss of half-a-million dollars. Many of the tenants were students from Southern Oregon State College who were out of town for the seasonal holidays. They were contacted and advised to take a few more days vacation.

The ground-level of three of the apartment buildings took water. One tenant said that the flood was more than four feet deep in her apartment and the only way she could leave was out the window as mud had jammed the door closed. Kirsten Ledous told the *Ashland Daily Tidings* she called 911 but could not get any immediate help so she called her parents in Portland. Soon, family connections and Jackson County authorities brought the

Ashland Creek tore out bridges, undercut pathways, ruined a playground and picnic areas.

Many beautiful Lithia Park shade trees fell victim first to being felled by the flood then to firewood-cutting chain saws.

cavalry in the form of the college wresting team. "Those guys got everything out [of the apartment]. We literally lost nothing."

Although damage to Lithia Park was primarily west of Ashland Creek, and at the north end of the park at Winburn Way, officials said park damage was not as extensive as it was in 1974. In the 1974 flood, all of the park's bridges were washed out and many of the rest rooms were damaged. In 1997, only one rest room was lost and 8 bridges, of 12, were lost. The Butler Band Shell sustained damage in 1974 but flood waters did not reach it in 1997.

On the north side of the Plaza, Bluebird Park was inundated by the flood. Although the little park no longer exists, much hope has been expressed that funds might be found to rebuild it. Water Street which runs alongside the little park, caved in due to the force of the flood and undermining of the pavement, which dropped nearly 20 feet leaving a large sink hole.

Paula Brown, an engineer with the Rogue Valley Council of Governments, stepped in to supervise operations and salvaging of the Talent water system. The town is served by two pumping stations. There is an older small pump on Wagner Creek above the town and the other, the main source, from a station on Bear

Websters The Handspinners Weavers & Knitters shop on the Plaza was "flooded and mudded" as the expression goes. Owners and volunteers hauled out everything that did not float down the creek. A de-humidifier was extracting about 10 gallons of water a day from the shop as much as two weeks later.

Creek. Both went out of order due to the flood. When the new pump is installed in the refurbished pump house on Bear Creek, one official said it should be named the "Paula Pump" for her work. (And it was. About three weeks later, a hand-made name plate, etched in wood, appeared at the pump house: PAULA PUMP.)

Muriel Johnson, owner of Tree House Books, planned to redecorate her store on the Plaza at the first of the year with the goal of reopening on January 10. She went to her place on December 31 and moved everything out in preparation for pulling up the carpet on the morrow. The rain had been coming down for days, Ashland Creek let go its fury and swamped her building, as it did every building on the Plaza. Johnson's loss was a worn-out carpet that had already been destined for discard. Because of the flood, she said her closure would take a little longer.

In Talent, it must have been like trying to salvage one's keepsakes after the skipper had cried, "Abandon ship." An elderly couple in their Joseph Street home were trying to save some furniture when their house tipped over and a part of it slipped under the water of flooding Wagner Creek. The house groaned, as is said a ship groans before taking the final plunge.

Next door, undermining of a house caused the deck to drop at a precarious angle into the water. How long the house will stand is a question. The City of Talent condemned six residences on that street but allows the owners 60 days for restoration or the city will tear them down as unsafe structures.

The flooding of lower Lithia Park and the Plaza apparently can be laid to the mud and boulders and fallen trees that rushed along swollen Ashland Creek from source areas just below Reeder reservoir. All this debris jammed the culvert that directs the creek under the lower park and under Winburn Way. To stop the runoff that inundated the Plaza and wrecked several businesses, took out Bluebird Park and collapsed Water Street, city crews struggled to place heavy equipment in Ashland Creek in the wee hours of January 1. Then they tore out the top of the culvert which forced the water to flow where it should be going and stop the "river" that was rushing through the Plaza. With a backhoe, the workers built a dike in the park to keep the water out of the Plaza.

Because a section of the access road to Reeder Reservoir was flooded out of existence, the Bonneville Power Administration (BPA) loaned a helicopter to lower a boat into the reservoir so inspectors could start clearing out floating debris from around the dam's spillways.

> **Grand Turn-Out**
> Over 300 volunteers showed up armed mostly with shovels and rakes for a Lithia Park cleanup day on January 18. They were supervised by Ashland Parks Department employees.

The large turnout of volunteers who wanted to help Ashland get back upon its feet was no less than amazing, according to the kudos observed by reading the "Letters to the Editor" columns in the Ashland and Medford papers. In addition, the vast majority of comments in the letters and those heard on the street praised city officials and the volunteers for jobs well done. One person was pretty upset that the water and toilets had been turned off and in her building none of the lights worked. But she

Heavy equipment played important role in saving the Plaza as the equipment was used to dig a wide channel through Winburn Way thus diverting the flood away from the Plaza.

declared, "The good old telephone. It always worked. Praise be to the telephone."

Jean Cook, writing in the *Ashland Daily Tidings* (January 16) said:

> While sympathizing deeply with those who have suffered severely, the majority of us were merely discommoded (pun intended) for about a week.

(TOP) **Flower Tyme and Ashland Fudge Company taking water under their front doors on January 1, 1997 from flooding Ashland Creek that escaped its banks and was roaring out of control through Ashland streets.** (LOWER) **Trash and mud from flooded shops, and mud scraped from street seen on January 7.**
—(TOP) Courtesy: R. Loren; (LOWER) author

In Central Point, where Griffin Creek ran amuck, the slop-over left between 18 and 36-inches of mud on one end – about 30 percent of the track – of the school's stadium. The school's Land Lab, an acreage on Bear Creek where students study vocational agriculture, was a mess and next to it, the district's Anhorn baseball field lost some land when Bear Creek changed its course. Vicki Robinson, the school district's business manager was quoted as saying the district maintained some pumps in the creek for watering the lawn at Anhorn Field but the pumps are nowhere to be found.

As the flood waters receded and victims had time to look around, advertisements started to show in the papers aimed toward helping them. One merchant hawked

> FLOOD VICTIMS - WE WANT TO HELP.
> SALE ON CARPET NO PAYMENT UNTIL 1998.

Another

> HOME DRYING AND DEHUMIDIFICATION
> FOR A LIMITED TIME ONLY

Another:

> FLOOD MERCHANDISE 25% - 60% OFF. CASH ONLY

Others:

> FLOOD VICTIM RELIEF
> FOR ASSISTANCE WITH FLOOD-DAMAGED ITEMS
> VISIT A RED CROSS SERVICE CENTER
> FOR COUPONS FOR DISCOUNTED DISPOSAL AT THE DUMP
>
> SEARS - WE'RE HERE TO HELP
>
> EMERGENCY FUNDS ARE HERE
> CALL WESTERN BANK FOR EMERGENCY ASSISTANCE
>
> MONTGOMERY WARD - WE'RE HERE TO HELP

Ashland suffered hurts due to the rain and flood, and the damage caused by both. It has happened before and there is no doubt that floods will happen again. But Ashland is a resilient city. It always bounces back quickly. ◇

Symbol of Lithia Park: The Swans

The leisurely swimming pair of swans in the pond in Lithia Park has brought thousands to the park just to see them. But when the flood roared through the park, barely missing the pond, one of the swans became confused and wandered off not necessarily because of the flood, but because this male swan had lost his mate in a dog attack nearly a year earlier. While wandering, the swan was hit by a truck while the truck was backing as part of the work in cleaning the Plaza of flood debris. Onlookers called out and the driver stopped the truck but it was too late. The dead swan was retrieved and later buried in the park.

Report of Damage Caused by Roca Creek
Extracted from Official Report to City of Ashland

Herman and Sylvia Schmeling reported the washout of 800 feet of cyclone fence, gates and posts between their place and Bear Creek caused by Roca and Bear Creeks at flood stage. The pasture was flooded from the east as Bear Creek overflowed and from the south when Roca Creek diverted from its normal channel and spread across a neighbor's property then washed over into the Schmeling pasture. He wrote:

Roca flooded our irrigation ditches bringing gravel and mud, leaves and debris with it plugging up pipes and causing overflow over railroad ties and sandbags. The lower pasture is a sea of mud, sand and gravel with water depth on the flood plain pasture between 6 and 24 inches.

This is at least the fourth time we have been flooded by overflows from Roca since 1991. When the new development went in above us, Roca Creek received runoff from new roofs, driveways and roads. Roca then overflowed into our irrigation ditches which had never been built to handle that much water. Result: flooding in our house and at our driveway. Neither in the flood of 1974, nor in any rainfall-caused flooding since then, did Roca Creek break through its banks as it did this time.

The estimated cost just to replace the fence, gates and posts runs to $3,200. Other repairs not yet quoted.

KOBI TV

Medford 5 M

Busy Night!
TV Cameramen Swims For His Life, Rescues Woman

While tooling along Interstate-5 in the station's Subaru "Justy" news-car, a reporter-videographer for KOBI-TV (5), James Sparks, suddenly realized his wheels were no longer on the pavement. His car was hydroplaning in several inches of water.

This was near the State weigh-station between the two Ashland exits at Butler Creek. As Sparks stopped the car, the Subaru nosed over and started down into what had become Butler "Lake." The driver, spotting his cell phone on the dash, grabbed it but could not open the door so he swiftly climbed out a window. In the flood, Sparks could not stand as the water was over his head so he swam to safety cell-phone in hand. The car disappeared from view as the water closed over it and his camera outfit.

Cell Phone Proves Worth

With the cellular-phone, he was calling newsman Chris Cochran at the station to report the incident when another car was broadsided then it too went into the "lake." Sparks jumped back into the water, swam to the wreck where he rescued the woman driver who required hospitalization.

It took two days to find the TV station's Subaru which had drifted about 300 yards down stream. The car was a total loss. The commercial TV camera, a Sony I-8, with a value of about $20,000, was also a total loss.

Sparks, who was the "on-call" reporter that night, had been on his way to the Medford studio for assignment when these incidents happened at about 3:15 on the morning of January 1.

Happy New Year!

Calle Guanajuato (Guanajuato Way) Hit Hard

Guanajuato Way is the short street that runs alongside Ashland Creek. It provides rear access doorways to a number of Plaza businesses and during summer months, artists and crafts people from around town display and sell their products in the Lithia Artisans Market on this street. During the New Year's Day 1997 flood, Calle Guanajuato was totally covered with the flooding Ashland Creek. Every business on the street suffered severe damage.

> (ABOVE) **Callé Guanajuato brightly decorated with the canopies of artisans during bright summer days.**
> (RIGHT PAGE) **Flooding Ashland Creek drowns the Callé on New Year's Day 1997.**
> —Flood photo courtesy: R. Loren. (INSET) author

Along the Callé Guanajuato: (TOP) bridge over Ashland Creek is washed away. (LOWER) Trash truck hauls debris from flooded area one week later.

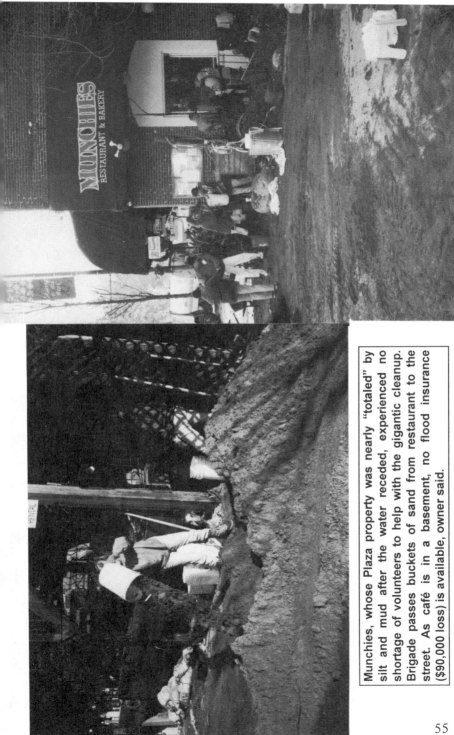

Munchies, whose Plaza property was nearly "totaled" by silt and mud after the water receded, experienced no shortage of volunteers to help with the gigantic cleanup. Brigade passes buckets of sand from restaurant to the street. As café is in a basement, no flood insurance ($90,000 loss) is available, owner said.

(TOP) **Chairs from Munchies stacked on Plaza to air-dry.** (LOWER) **Contaminated citrus fruit and other debris from basements of Callé shops.**

(TOP) **Sand is heavy and it is a tough job heaving a loaded wheelbarrow up a steep ramp to the street. But somebody had to do it.** (LOWER) **Portable water pumps were in short supply throughout Ashland.**

Red Cross Emergency Response Vehicle (ERV) at Ashland Plaza offered mid-morning hot coffee and snacks to volunteer workers. Temperature was 29°F. (LOWER) Ashland policewoman picks up cup of coffee which she carried to a worker who was about a block away.

American Red Cross – Chartered by Congress

The American Red Cross and the Jackson County Emergency Operating Center announced that volunteer response has been "absolutely fantastic" resulting in pages and pages of signups by people who want to be helpful because of the flood.

> The most heartening news to come out of the flood was that there were no deaths and only a few minor injuries.

The major need was for shelter, food and drinking water and personal care. By January 4th, the Red Cross had served 803 meals and cared for 243 persons in shelters. Initial shelters included the gym at Southern Oregon State College, Phoenix High School, Talent Community Hall and the Medford National Guard Armory.

Fred Meyer supermarkets, Culligan Water Service were quick to donate bottled water.

Farmers who had backhoes and tractors with blades were in demand for digging and shoving flood-mud from streets.

The Red Cross distributed hundreds of Disaster Cleanup Kits. Each kit included a heavy broom, shovel, and other tools.

As for hot food, the American Red Cross Disaster Services fleet of trucks are rushed to where ever they are needed, we were told. Trucks are based in strategic places throughout the United States, and there is one garaged in Medford, Oregon. On a moment's notice, trucks, each with a crew of two volunteer drivers, can be dispatched to a needed site. For the New Year's Day 1997 flood in and around Ashland, the American Red Cross dispatched two trucks from as far away as Kansas City, Missouri, driven across the country by two "more-than-middle-age women drivers." Workers also arrived from Iowa and New Jersey.

Juniper Baptist Association, Bend, Oregon, Southern Baptist Convention Disaster Relief, volunteered its response truck with portable propane cookstoves, to the Red Cross for the New Year's Day 1997 flood. Field kitchen was set up behind National Guard Armory in Medford. Unit cooked hundreds of appetizing meals, with shifts working night and day.

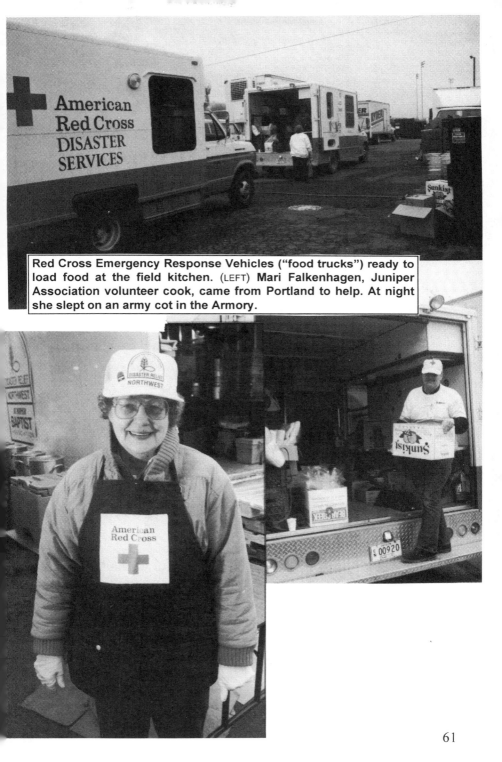

Red Cross Emergency Response Vehicles ("food trucks") ready to load food at the field kitchen. (LEFT) Mari Falkenhagen, Juniper Association volunteer cook, came from Portland to help. At night she slept on an army cot in the Armory.

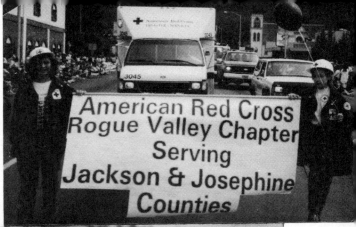

Many forced out of homes sought refuge in Red Cross emergency shelters. This one in Medford National Guard Armory. Checkers was a popular game, as well as cards. There were coloring books for the kids and free Pepsi and hot coffee.
—Top photo from American Red Cross, Medford. Lower: —author

Health and Safety Precautions

Do not turn on electrical appliances that were flooded

Eat from paper plates and throw-away plastic utensils

Electric heaters and electric hot water tanks should be disconnected or the circuit breakers thrown or fuses removed

Food - canned. If not punctured or puffed, wash cans in mix of 2 teaspoons of chlorine in one gallon of water

Food - fresh. Throw out fresh foods that have been in contact with flood waters

Gas operated hot water tanks should be turned to "pilot light only" but do not shut off gas at the meter

People staying in their homes need to establish a discipline of careful hand washing and drinking and cooking and brushing teeth using only water known-to-be-safe

Persons with cuts or scratches that get wet in flood waters should see a physician to consider a tetanus booster

Toilets: Turn off water intake valve at the wall. Flush with rainwater that has been poured into the tank. A 10-quart bucket of water will usually flush a toilet.

Toilets: Use chemical toilets if available.

Washing dishes: Use one capful of liquid bleach in a sink of water. Let utensils stand in this mixture for up to 5 minutes. Air dry.

Water: use none from streams or rivers.

Wear boots and gloves when walking in flood water as the water might contain sewage. Watch out for hazardous matter that might be floating or be submerged in the flood

Well water: Boil it and strain it. Treat with chlorine until a test is completed by competent laboratory.

As the refugee-public learned that the relief was at hand, meals dispensed quickly ran to over 3,000. These meals are not just "'MRE' – pre-packaged 'Meals Ready to Eat' from the Gulf War – or good old baloney and peanut butter sandwiches," declared Rick Boalister, a man displaced by the flood. "These meals may be Spanish rice, chili-mac, cut jumbo franks and beans, or that great beef stew" he continued. (Fresh green salads and local freshly baked buns also make up parts of menus.)

Because there was much anxiety about how to cope with a disaster, the American Red Cross sponsored several forums for flood victims on how to handle stress caused by the flood.

Dean Harris, a Disaster Mental Health Officer of the Red Cross, said,

A large flood ... challenges our ability to respond to everyday problems by overwhelming our typical coping mechanisms. People often either deny the stress they are experiencing or feel their symptoms are signs of disorder. Both are often actually normal reactions to abnormal events.

He posted a list of some typical delayed responses to a disaster:

Anger and suspicion	Frustration and feeling powerless
Anxiety about the future	Guilt about being unable to prevent the disaster
Apathy	
Crying for no apparent reason	Headaches
Depression	Increased effects of allergies
Difficulty sleeping	Irritability
Domestic violence	Isolating from friends and family
Feeling overwhelmed	Moodiness
	Nightmares
	Rejection of outside help

Children suffer special effects which may include:
- Bed-wetting
- Clinging to parents
- Crying
- Fantasies that a disaster didn't happen
- Inability to concentrate in school
- Nightmares
- Refusing to go to school
- Reluctance to go to bed
- Screaming
- Sleeplessness
- Thumb-sucking
- Withdrawal and immobility

"They [the Red Cross] are here when you need them," said a grandmotherly type who had just lost her mobile home that had been in a trailer park that was flooded.* ◇

---

* See Appendix for an historical sketch of the American Red Cross. —Editor

The Salvation Army – Always Ready

Captain Robert Roome, Salvation Army, and Wayne Hutchcroft, a staff member at the Salvation Army office in Medford, were contacted by a friend of two families whose trailers had just been swamped by the flooding Bear Creek at Jackson Hot Springs Trailer Park. This was on the first day of the flood, January 1, 1997. The Salvation Army had already mobilized its forces and were answering telephone pleas for help.

As this relief agency maintains a list of available vacant apartments and houses, it offered one of the vacant apartments for the refugees to live in then immediately supplied beds, bedding and various other basic necessities.

The Salvation Army is a "behind the scenes" operation, explained Mick Johnson, the Medford Social Services Supervisor.

As the flood disaster increased, we immediately donated clean-up materials to the Red Cross, which could be passed along to flood victims to allow the people to clean up their muddied homes. The cleanup kits we had on hand had been stored after a smaller flood last year.

The kit is a carton containing a mop, broom, bucket, dustpan, sponge, cleaning materials (detergent, germicidal solution), hand scrub brush and plastic trash bags.

This agency also has a fully-rigged trailer, their "canteen," which can be towed by a car or pickup to a disaster site. The canteen is arranged to serve hot meals as well as hand out emergency supplies to those in need. The trailer, always kept stocked and ready-to-go, was offered to the Red Cross but its use was not requested.

On the second day of the flood, six families appeared at the Ashland Salvation Army Thrift Store seeking food and blankets saying they would be staying with family and friends for the time being. The requests were met at no cost to those displaced.

The floods were not only in Ashland, but were throughout

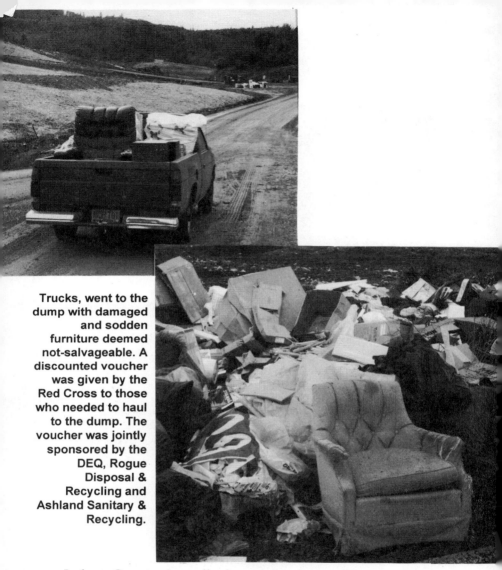

Trucks, went to the dump with damaged and sodden furniture deemed not-salvageable. A discounted voucher was given by the Red Cross to those who needed to haul to the dump. The voucher was jointly sponsored by the DEQ, Rogue Disposal & Recycling and Ashland Sanitary & Recycling.

Jackson County. Accordingly, people whose welfare was hurt by the disaster appeared at the Ashland and the Medford offices from many areas of the county. These included Ashland's Jackson Hot Springs and Nauvoo Trailer Parks, Medford, Lake Creek and Eagle Point. The emergency needs of many from Nauvoo and from Bear Lake Mobile Estates was so severe that a number of these folks were sent to the Medford Thrift Store which is larger.

There was a delightful lady from Butte Creek who had lost everything. People came from the flooded units at Barnett Townhouses at Ellendale and Barnett Road in Medford where Larson Creek was the culprit.

> **The Salvation Army, which never charges for any item provided during a disaster, paid for an urgently needed bus ticket out of town for a person stranded by the flood; helped with some utility bills that had to be paid due to sudden flood-forced unemployment; provided a willing ear to many who were frustrated with the emergency and needed to vent their anger. "We listen, we smile a lot, and we try our best to have the person leave in a better spirit than when he came in – and we don't 'preach' at anybody," Mick Johnson related.**

Many people take responsibility for their hurting neighbors and volunteer to help when a need arises. Nanci Caster, who operates the Ashland Salvation Army Thrift Store, received donations of clothing, canned groceries, bedding and furniture right from the start of the disaster. Johnson related:

> Every donated item that is provided by the public for use in the disaster, is given freely to those in need. None of these donations ever go into our Thrift Stores for sale.

Caster received donations, sorted them, routed used clothing to the Medford center for laundering, then distributed these gifts as needed. In the first 10 days of the flood, the Ashland Thrift Store provided food boxes, personal hygiene items, clothing, cleaning supplies and blankets for 43 families. At one point, the store ran out of free sofas and beds and had to send folks to the Medford store.

When the flood finally gave up and those merchants who had been flooded out of their business locations had a combined "flood salvage sale" in a shopping center, the Salvation Army Ashland Thrift Store loaned clothes racks and display tables from the store to be helpful.

On January 28, nearly a month after the start of the New Year's Day 1997 flood, Nanci Caster, and her staff, was still generously handing out Salvation Army emergency food boxes, clothing and blankets.

Many mops, buckets, brooms, brushes, shovels and cleaning agents were given away by Red Cross and by Salvation Army.

A volunteer with the Red Cross remarked that the Red Cross was chartered as the official emergency national disaster relief agency by the Congress of the United States. This prompted a member of the Salvation Army to retort: "We operate by charter from a higher authority." *◇

---

* See Appendix for an historical sketch of the Salvation Army. —Editor

Main Street (Highway 99) at the Plaza in Ashland was closed due to the flood on New Year's Day. A visitor from New York declared, "This is a mess."
—Courtesy: R. Loren

(TOP) When the Plaza flooded, merchants on Main Street sand bagged their doorways as how high up the inclined street the water would seep was unknown. (LOWER) On the Plaza, less than one block downhill, many loads of damaged merchandise was wheeled out of the shops then to the dump.

On New year's Day, this was the scene of a mini-Niagara Falls as racing flood waters from Ashland Creek, by way of the Plaza, caused Water Street (shown) to collapse. The flood also took out adjacent Bluebird Park.

Many business houses rented chemical toilets for the benefit of their customers and their employees.

Street Corner Toileting
It's Still a Privy Even if It's Made of Yellow Plastic

The matter of the chemical toilets on the streets in Ashland and in Talent brought a deluge of comments on broadcast call-in shows and in letters to the editors of the papers. And the papers did feature stories about those oddities which people found perched around town: Porta-potties, also called "chemical toilets." One company placed close to 200 out-houses in business houses and for homeowners. Another contracted to put another 100 on the streets, sponsored by the city, plus another 100 elsewhere.

Some ladies complained of not wanting to be seen entering the stalls so some did their best to await darkness. Some were upset that earlier user(s) failed to put the seat down. Others complained about the fragrance. Many were disappointed on discovering it was dark in there after nightfall, "no electric lights." (Depending on material used in making some privies, it is dark inside day or night.) One commentator on a news broadcast pleaded with users to be sure to bring their own toilet paper. A woman, on emerging and facing a line of "waiters," declared in a loud voice: "Men! Why do they pee on the seat"? A woman,

A line of bright yellow plastic monsters in front of Ashland's Safeway Store. One lady complained, "They could have at least faced the doors away from the gawking traffic on Siskiyou Boulevard."

dressed in a fur coat (it was cold that morning), complained that there were no "gaskets." One was quite upset to discover that in addition to no lights, there was no heat.

On January 4, 1997, the Medford *Mail Tribune* headlined a story, "Porta-Potties: The Insult After Injury."

One of the more unique mini-feature stories of the day could have been written (better in movies) about the case of the chauffeur-driven limousine and the two elderly women. We learned that each day about 6 a.m., again about 11, then at 3, 7 and 10 p.m. – a daily schedule – the driver delivered the ladies in the shining 20-foot long vehicle to the line of yellow potties that were in front of the Safeway Store. He parked near the end of the lineup where the women emerged, then walked in a business-like manner looking neither to the left nor to the right, each entering the two end "facilities." As soon as the two doors clicked shut, the driver dashed to the closet on the other end of the line and in a relatively short time emerged then dashed back to the limousine where he took his position standing at a rear door to await his passengers.

The line of "yellow monsters," as one person called them, got most of the newspaper and TV attention because of the

Some folks had to walk, even drive, blocks to the nearest street corner "Throne Room." Some dubbed their visits as "The Pause That Refreshes," a slogan borrowed from Coca Cola. Regrettably, vagrants stole a lot of the toilet paper.

Portable Toilets Were Placed at These Principal Ashland Locations:

Albertson's Market
Ashland Community Food Store
Ashland High School
Ashland Middle School
Bellview Elementary School
Bi-Mart Department Store
Brisco Elementary School
Buy-Rite Market

Cantwell's Market
Helman Elementary School
Lincoln Elementary School
National Guard Armory
Safeway Market
Walker Elementary School

➔ Dozens of additional chemical toilets were set up throughout the town including a line of them in front of the Elizabethan Theater.

This squad of privies, painted blue, did duty in front of the Elizabethan Theater

IMPORTANT NOTICE

Please do NOT place filled plastic bags in these facilities. You may dispose contents of plastic portapotty liners in here, but you MUST take the liner BACK with you.

bright color which looked good in pictures. But there were also other colors. One wag observed that the Shakespeare-oriented "blue-bloods" could not bring themselves to use the "yellow monsters" but went to the Elizabethan Theater, where, in front of the main doors, was a line of portable privies painted blue.

One Christmas, a son gave his mother what he labeled as "The World's Largest Coffee Cup." Although he didn't know it, his gift was an antique thunder-mug. The woman told us:

> For years this 'cup' has been in my den with flowers in it. But with the restrictions imposed during the flood, I dusted off this antique and indeed I had it ready, should I need it for its intended purpose.

When it became apparent that many persons had porta-potties in their campers, and were using them then carrying the potty-liners (plastic bags) to the corner facilities for "deposit," the vendors posted large-print notices on all toilet doors saying that dumping the contents of the bags was OK, but the persons would have to carry the fragrant bags away with them.

While hundreds were glad that the chemical toilets had been made available because using one beat having to sneak into the bushes, a letter writer summed up the reaction of many to the temporary corner closets:

1). The perfume emitted was "ghastly"
2). The facility had no lights
3). One was unsure of the door's lock
4). The closets were claustrophobic
5). "Every time I stepped out of one, people on the street were looking at me"
6). "In the middle of the night the seats were ice cold. When I got sat, I lost the urge."

One letter pointed out:

> People did not voice how happy they were that their lives had been spared because there were no outbreaks of cholera or dysentery due to somebody's quick decision to set up dozens of portable closets on street corners. Thanks to 'Somebody.'

A grandmotherly type waited outside the door for her turn and remarked almost fondly, "Except that this one is painted bright yellow, this reminds me of the privy I grew up with in Arkansas over 70 year ago." ◇

Hospital Safe – Is On High Ground

Portable toilets, gallon jugs of drinking water for in-hospital use, and a National Guard tanker in the parking lot for nearby residents....

The first Ashland baby of 1997 was born January 1 at 6:21 in the morning in Ashland Community Hospital. She is Dylan Owens and weights 8 lbs. 12 oz. The parents, Lynette and Micah Owens had planned a natural birth delivery at their home in the mountains, on Cove Road some miles from town, but as the storm became heavier, they decided to head for the hospital. Later, the mother, Lynette Owens declared, "If we hadn't gone to the hospital, we'd be stuck up there. The house was fine, but there is a huge gorge across the road now."

At the hospital, about the only difference in a day's operation was that meals came to patients on paper plates and there were no showers. As for the toilets, city officials said "OK" for patients to use toilets but employees would have to use the portable privy outdoors.

The hospital keeps at least a week's food on hand in case of an emergency. Early in the emergency, Lenny Friedman, who owns Ashland's Pyramid Juice Company, made an interstate dash to the Yreka, California WAL-MART to obtain 200 bottles of water. Then an order for 4,000 gallons was delivered from Safeway. But these were temporary measures.

Question: How much water would it take for 150 employees to wash their hands 30 times? Arrangements were made for Marie's Water Service to park a tank of 5,000 gallons at the hospital.

Help came from Medford, where fresh water was plentiful, for the hospital's tank to be filled by Medford tankers.

Community effort and cooperation from neighbors kept Ashland Community Hospital open and ready for medical emergencies that might come in from the flood zones. None did. ◇

Emigrant Lake Dam
and the Talent Irrigation District

Hollie Cannon, Secretary and Manager for the Talent Irrigation District, told us that the weather bureau forecasts on December 30 led him to take immediate action concerning the district's dam which forms Emigrant Lake (2,174 feet elevation). The dam and lake are four miles southeast of Ashland. On that date, the storage of Emigrant Lake was 4,447 acre-feet above the flood course due to an earlier storm. Discharge was 400 cubic feet per second (cfs). The developing storm caused Cannon to stop discharge. At the peak of storage, the release had been 4 cfs and the lake was within twelve hours of having water runoff over the emergency overflow spillway. The lake stores a maximum of 39,000 acre feet and was nearing 5,000 feet of that capacity when discharge began. Input into the lake had been high for over a week due to melting snow and the continuous rain.

BEAR CREEK FLOW DECEMBER 30, 1996 - JAN 1, 1997
US BUREAU OF RECLAMATION - PN470 BOISE JAN 7 1997 MFDO Q EMI Q

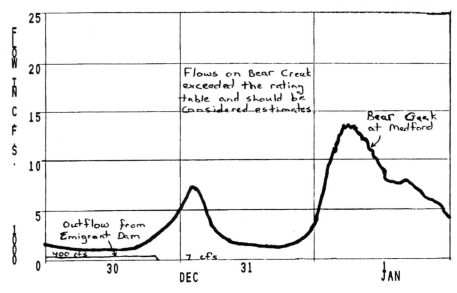

The project authorization by Congress approved Emigrant Reservoir for irrigation, flood control and for benefits to fish and wildlife.

On December 30, about 7 p.m., Cannon shut off the outflow gates at the dam to where only about 7 cfs of water was escaping. By 2 a.m. December 31, the peak flow of Bear Creek was 7,000 cfs and dropped by mid-day to about 2,000 cfs. On January 1, 1997, a little after midnight, the creek was again on the rise and by 3 a.m., the peak of about 13,000 cfs was reached, with a high of about 12,000 cfs at Medford by mid-morning.

By midnight January 1, the creek's flow had dropped to about 4,000 cfs. Cannon said if there had been no dam to check the water, the flow would have been 22,000 cfs resulting in "double damage in the valley below."* He pointed out that "flows on Bear Creek exceeded the rating table and would be considered estimates."◇

---

* The first dam to create the source of water for the Talent Irrigation District was built about 1926, then the dam was enlarged (raised 30 feet) in 1956. Cannon reported that the Bureau of Reclamation does a detailed inspection of the dam at three-year intervals and last reported the dam to be in excellent condition.

Emigrant Creek runs out of the mountains southeast of Ashland. The reservoir is commonly called Emigrant Lake on which there is a camping park and extensive water sports in summer months. The outflow from the reservoir retains the name Emigrant Creek until its water makes confluence with Ashland Creek at a point northwest of Ashland where the combined creeks become Bear Creek. According to McArthur, writing in *Oregon Geographic Names,* the name "emigrant" was from the fact that emigrants on the Applegate Trail, a branch of the Oregon Trail, followed this creek in 1846 into what was called the Rogue River Valley. The name Rogue River Valley is a misnomer as the Rogue River is about 25-miles to the north. Many consider the cities of Ashland, Talent, Phoenix, Medford and Central Point to be in the Bear Creek Valley.

Bear Creek was originally called Stuart Creek for nearby short-lived Camp Stuart, a military post set up during the Rogue Indian War. The creek was named for Captain Jack Stuart who died June 18, 1851 after losing a skirmish with Indians. McArthur says settlers changed the creek's name to Bear Creek, for an unrecorded reason.

Picture from Bear Lake Mobile Estates

Mobile Homes - Trailers No Match for Flood

For the most part, a mobile home is perched on concrete blocks, or sometimes, especially older models, may rest on its

← Picture on facing page
Bear Lake Mobile Estates Across Bear Creek Viewed from Interstate-5

The park, on Luman Road, Phoenix, contained 210 mobile homes. Ten were damaged and can be repaired but 73 were rendered unlivable by the flooding Bear Creek and were classed as totally destroyed. In one home where the flood left a clearly defined stain-line, the water had risen to 32-inches.

One owner reported his loss at $51,000 for the mobile home, $50,000 in personal property including a totally destroyed 1982 Cadillac car, and his prized Chickering piano. The piano was salvaged but the strings had rusted. He said the piano will require, in addition to new strings, a total rebuild at about $6,500. He was one of a few who had pre-planned. He had flood insurance.

Crest Imperial Estates, a trailer park on Ellendale Drive in Medford, took full force of raging Bear Creek. Mobile home shown was twisted about 90 degrees off its foundation next to concrete parking pad by force of the water. Trailer was condemned by city.

Many mobile homes in Crest Imperial Estates were twisted from their mounts and some totally wrecked from further occupancy.

transport wheels. So-called regular trailers, including 5th wheel models, stand on their wheels and on a stud in front near the tow-bar.

If the unit is parked temporarily or permanently in a parking place within a flood plain, in the local case, too close to Bear Creek, or the Rogue River, then the unit is at extremely high risk of being upset and possibly destroyed if hit by a sudden swollen creek or river. Such was the case during the New year's Day 1997 flood.

Bear Creek is a traditional "flooder" in winter and in some years the creek runs higher than others. When a flood hits, mobile homes and trailers might be lifted off their perches or wheels and carried downstream to be twisted and broken in the rushing waters then piled into a heap against some obstruction. Such was the case during the New year's Day 1997 flood.

Why are trailer parks established so close to unpredictable streams? One suggested reason is that the cost of the land, being within a flood plain, is low cost and a building permit could not

DO NOT ENTER – UNSAFE BUILDING signs went on several wrecked mobile homes at Crest Imperial Estates. In picture, Bear Creek is less than 20 yards away.

be obtained for a permanent buildings such as homes in the risk area. It may be nice to park a trailer under the shade trees along a creek in summer and be sung to sleep nights with the gurgle of the creek. But come rainy season, it would seem to be the time to move to higher ground. Unfortunately, too many mobile home and trailer owners have not kept these factors in mind.

Weather forecasters can sometimes predict a forthcoming rip-roaring creek-raising rain storm, but sometimes the notice is very short. The pattern of weather that develops on land is determined by the winds aloft – the jet-stream and its whip-saw action. When the winds carry moist tropical air then dumps its load in the Pacific Northwest, flooding in a particular area might be predicted by watching the path of the jet-stream. If the whipping current of air, which is often 30,000 to 50,000 feet altitude, passes over the North American landfall in a place different from Southern Oregon, then the rain will hit somewhere else and rivers and creeks in that area are likely to flood. Although there

(TOP) **Once a nice planted area with dog warning sign, this yard now just a mud heap caused by the flood at Bear Lake Mobile Estates.**
(LOWER) **Force of flood-driven trees and rocks knocked over street signs and bent the poles. Shown is Callé Guanajuato in Ashland.**

were floods throughout the Pacific Northwest at the turn of the year, the dumping ground for much of the jet stream's moisture was in Southern Oregon. ◇

Police Blotter

Police and Fire Departments in the southern end of the Rogue River Valley (Phoenix, Talent, Ashland) made few arrests as the forces abandoned usual patrols to help persons displaced by the flood and to direct traffic.

Ashland police rescued persons isolated in the upper floor in apartments at 15 Winburn Way, as the occupants' escape was blocked by raging flood waters at their front door.

Nauvoo Trailer Park, North Pacific Highway, across from the Ford and Chevy dealerships was especially hard hit.

A few miles away in Phoenix, the Police arrested two people for trespass and theft in an area that had been evacuated due to flooding.

Ashland Police, assisted by volunteers, patrolled the Plaza to prevent trespassing and stealing.

Please Do Not Park on the Grass

Nauvoo

Nauvoo Mobile Estates is on the flood plain of Bear Creek, is immediately next to the creek. Flood devastated the site. Photographs made January 7, 1977 by authors

Nauvoo

(TOP) **Lunches, provided from visiting Red Cross emergency vehicle, find volunteer workers where ever they could find a place to sit to eat. The hot lunch this day was beef stew, fresh rolls, tossed green salad.** (LOWER) **In the midst of the site is fresh water station. Water to drink; water to wash hands.**

Nauvoo

(TOP) **One of the first items to be stripped from flooded homes was carpet. Shown is pile of carpet that will eventually go to the dump for which the Red Cross distributed discount dump coupons to those who needed them.** (LOWER) **Regardless of what was in the way of the flood, it was probably smashed, including this metal picnic table/bench set. (See bent street sign on page 85.)**

Talent Police patrolled premises at Oregon RV Roundup, a trailer park on the edge of town and on the bank of Bear Creek as the creek rose (TOP) threatening the park. — Photo courtesy of Don Squires. In the middle of the night, an evacuation order was given and all vehicles moved out to the nearest place to go, the Wal-Mart parking lot across the creek. (LOWER) In the morning, when store workers arrived for work, they were amazed to see their lot full "road whales." The RV park expects an uninsured loss of close to $300,000 and to permanently lose 22 sites.
—Photo courtesy of Yvonne Rowe

Bear Creek Greenway's bike and hiking path was inundated here by the flood. Path, heavily enjoyed by folks from nearby RV parks, is total loss with repairs delayed until various government agencies assess priorities.

Holiday RV Park, Phoenix, was baptized in flood waters that rose to nearly 2 feet above the 10-foot marker on the adjacent highway bridge. Park was evacuated with many rigs moving across the freeway to temporary refuge at Pear Tree Truck Stop. Damage to the RV park was estimated at nearly $100,000.

Dorothea Phillips, U S WEST telephone installer, has her hands full restoring service at Holiday RV Park a week after the waters subsided.

Raging Rogue River, south of gorge near Union Creek
—Courtesy: Preston Mitchell

Hooray!
Rogue River Gorge Choked For Decades With Debris, Cleared by New Year's Day 1997 Flood

It was hard to imagine there was a real river down there, the view clogged so heavily with fallen timber all these years. But with the power of the flooded river roaring along its steep route and moving like a rolling freight train going down-hill without brakes, the flood carried with it decades of debris and fallen timber.

One can now see the river and the sight is spectacular.

The Gorge of the Rogue River is within the Rogue River National Forest and can be viewed across from Union Creek Resort on High way 62. The river actually flows through a collapsed lava tube believed to have been created with the volcanic collapse of Mt. Mazama eons ago. The phenomena of the gorge at this point in the river has been seen by thousands of visitors. ◇

Flood Control
U. S. Army Corps of Engineers

A Rouge River flood control master plan adopted many years ago envisioned a brace of three dams. These were Lost Creek Dam on the Rogue River, about 45 miles northeast of Medford, Applegate Dam on the Applegate River about 30 miles southwest of Medford, and Elk Creek Dam on Elk Creek, near the town of Trail about midway between Lost Creek Dam and Medford. The Elk Creek dam site is 27 miles from Medford.

The major dam was Lost Creek. Environmentalists fought bitterly to kill the entire project but Lost Creek and Applegate Dams survived the hassles. Lost Creek Dam was finished in 1977 and Applegate followed in 1980. Elk Creek Dam became an environmentalist target – an all-out effort to stop that project right up to a point when it was about half built, when a court order stopped the work. One report claims the contractor was paid off with nearly enough money to have finished the dam. Presently, Elk Creek slithers its way through the unfinished monument of concrete. All three of these dams were primarily flood-control projects.

Gene G. Rushing, writing a Letter to the Editor in the *Mail Tribune* (January 10,. 1977) said he hoped the folks who worked against finishing Elk Creek Dam will contribute to the disaster fund to help the victims of the flood. He asks, "How much worse would it have been without Lost Creek and Applegate dams"? Rushing reminded that millions were spend on a dam (Elk Creek) that can't be used and now millions more for repairs along the Rogue River. He concludes, "Is it any wonder so many people feel as if the inmates are running the asylum"?

Speaking of the New Year's Day 1997 flood, a Corps of Engineers spokesman declared that "we captured a major chunk of the flood at the dam sites." During the 1997 storm, the two dams caught and held more water from a single storm system than ever before. Lost Creek Lake recorded runoff at 26,200 cubic feet per second (cfs) at 3 p.m. on Jan 1 and the dam held all but 2,000 cfs.

Grants Pass residential area flooded severely in the 1964 flood. — Author collection from U. S. Army Corps of Engineers

> Enough water was kept in Lost Creek Dam in one hour to cover downstream ground the size of 100 football fields with a flood 18 feet deep.

On the Applegate River, the dam kept enough water to delay the river's crest at 17 feet, four feet above flood stage, nearly eight hours, at the village of Applegate. Some flooding occurred at the town which one spokesman suggested might plausibly have been wiped out except for the dam.

On the Rogue River, had Elk Creek Dam been finished and "doing its thing holding water back," the flooding at Dodge Bridge, where there is a key measuring station, and in the flat lands near Central Point, and elsewhere downstream, might well have been avoided. ◇

Earlier Floods

The 1890 and 1892 floods swamped E. Main Street in Medford near Hawthorne Park and forced a run-off ditch in Hawthorne Park nearly twenty feet wide and about four feet deep.

Feb. 20, 1927 flood. Bear Creek, carrying debris, clogged Cottage Street Bridge (Medford) so Street Department men dynamited the bridge.

Southern Pacific stopped southbound trains at Grants Pass and northbound trains at Dunsmuir after part of the rain-swollen roof in Tunnel 13, under Siskiyou Summit, caved in. During the heavy rain, about 100 passengers, from a train stuck at Medford, were treated to a dance at the depot. The railroad was obligated to feed them, then rent overnight accommodations for everyone.

Medford attorney Jeannette Marshall remembers a flood of Bear Creek, plausibly in winter 1938 or 1939. She was a student at Southern Oregon Normal School (presently Southern Oregon State College), and went home to Medford on week-ends. On the weekend of memory she recalled:

> Bear Creek was so high that it washed out a fox farm, located in a low area just north of Jackson Hot Springs. I do not remember the Hot Springs having any trouble with high water that year, but the fox farm was totaled and never did go back into business.

As a result of the 1974 flooding when damage to streets was pegged at $1,000,000, Ashlanders passed a bond issue of $400,000 to fix the streets with the rest coming from the federal government.

Reeder Reservoir is the source of fresh water for Ashland. It is in the Siskiyou Mountains at 2,870 feet elevation in Ashland Creek Canyon, and gets its water from the Ashland Watershed, a protected area of 14,425 acres within the Rogue River National Forest. The dam was first called Reeder Gulch Dam. The dam was built in 1928, is moon-shaped and is of reinforced concrete. The dam is 103-feet high and when full, its reservoir will hold 277,000,000 gallons of water. The dam was formally named the Hosler Dam for the late Earl R. Hosler who had been a superintendent of the Ashland Water Department. But the dam and reservoir is usually just referred to as Reeder reservoir and dam.

The reservoir has three prime methods of access. 1.) Hike. 2.) Rural road. 3.) Helicopter. During the New Year's Day 1997 Flood, the best access was by helicopter as the flood washed out the access road.

At Wagner Creek, which bisects Talent, questions came up with people trying to understand the difference, if there was any difference, between earlier floods and the 1997 disaster.

A county survey technician said that for years Wagner Creek has always returned to its basic channel after floods as far back as 1912, when the county started its record. But in the January 1, 1997 flood, Wagner Creek changed its channel in its lower regions. Why?

A state lands inspector observed that land development replaces vegetation-covered ground with thousands of square feet of roofs on buildings and paved roads, "asphalt jungles," which have taken away natural vegetation which could hold rain-soaked soil in place. Another factor is logging operations high in the hills.

In Southwestern Oregon, winter storms have historically brought the largest floods compared to sudden summer thunderstorms. For Ashland Creek, the major potential troublemaker for the City of Ashland, severe flooding happened in 1853, 1861, 1890, 1955, 1964, 1974 and in January 1997.

These floods happened due to heavy rain soaking the snow packs on the mountain causing the snow to melt then combined with more rain, the run-off drained into creeks which became flooded. In lower elevations, the creeks overflowed their banks.

The rain-on-snow phenomenon happens usually between about 3,500 feet and 5,000 feet elevation which is about 40 percent of the Ashland watershed. Another 25 percent is above 5,000 feet. In that upper elevation, precipitation is usually snow. In the snow areas, the usual melt is over several months time in spring and early summer putting smaller amounts of water in the creeks. Mt. Ashland, 7,533 feet elevation, is not snow-covered the year around as is Mt. Shasta, 14,162 feet elevation southeast of Ashland. The rest of the Ashland watershed is under 3,500 feet where snow falls more lightly and seldom sticks for more

Worst Recorded Floods. Rogue River.
Measurements at Grants Pass

Date		Stage		Flow	
Dec.	*1861*	--		*175,000 cfs**	*(estimated)*
Feb.	*1890*	--		*160,000 cfs**	*(estimated)*
Feb.	*1907*	--		*60,500 cfs*	*(estimated)*
Nov.	*1909*	--		*70,000 cfs*	*(estimated)*
Feb.	*1927*	--		*138,000 cfs**	*(estimated)*
Dec.	*1942*	--		*54,400 cfs*	
Dec	*1945*	--		*70,000 cfs*	
Jan.	*1948*	--		*59,900 cfs*	
Oct.	*1950*	--		*65,400 cfs*	
Jan.	*1953*	--		*77,000 cfs*	
Dec.	*1955*	--		*135,000 cfs**	
Dec. 23, 1964		31.15 ft		152,000 cfs*	
Jan. 27, 1970		20.2	ft	59,000 cfs	
Jan. 17, 1971		25.8	ft	87,000 cfs*	
Jan. 22, 1972		24.6	ft	81,000 cfs	
Mar 2, 1972		24.9	ft	82,500 cfs	
Jan 14, 1974		27.5	ft	96,000 cfs*	
Mar. 18, 1975		19.5	ft	56,000 cfs	
Dec. 19, 1981		23.1	ft	79,000 cfs	
Dec. 18, 1983		23.1	ft	73,000 cfs	
Jan. 1, 1997		25.55 ft		85,830 cfs*	

* cfs: Cubic Feet per second. Most noted floods
—Data from National Weather Service – Medford, Oregon Office
—*Data in italic is from U.S. Army Corps of Engineers - Portland*

than a few days.

Two major floods in most people's memory, previous to the New Year's Day 1997 flood, were in 1964 and 1974. The 1964 flood has been called "The Christmas Week Flood," but the most of it was the week before Christmas. That flood covered much of the western part of the country from Washington into Southern California. For the Rogue River Valley, the 1964 flood was the highest on record.

The 1974 flood was about the same as the flood 10 years

Historical River Stage Data – Rogue River – Grants Pass
Statistics between 1862 — 1983
Elevation: 884.28 feet

(Rounded)	(Remarks)	(Actual)	(Date)	
43.0 ft	**Highest flood on record**	**43.00 ft**	Jan. 1,	1862
41.0	Measured at floor of pump house	41.00	No date	
36.0	Measured at Highway 99 bridge floor	36.00	Feb. 1,	1890
35.15	No recorded data	35.15	Dec. 23,	1964
33.6	Severe primary bank erosion right bank from 6th St. to west city limits	33.60	Dec. 22,	1955
32.0	No recorded data	32.00	Feb. 21,	1927
30.0	Major flooding, many farms and residences on lower banks from Savage Rapids Dam to mouth of Applegate, particularly left bank near Grants Pass		No date	
28.0	No recorded data	28.30	Dec. 2,	1962
27.5	No recorded data	27.90	Jan. 18,	1953
27.0	No recorded data	27.20	Dec. 29,	1945
	No recorded data	25.88	Jan. 16,	1974
	No recorded data	25.30	Aug. 29,	1950
	No recorded data	25.20	Nov. 13,	1953
	No recorded data	25.17	Jan. 17,	1971
	No recorded data	24.20	Mar. 2,	1972
	No recorded data	23.89	Dec. 31,	1942
	No recorded data	23.20	Jan, 28,	1954
	No recorded data	22.88	Feb. 18,	1983
21.0	Slight lowland flooding downstream of Highway 99 bridge along River Rd.		No date	
	No recorded data	20.80	Jan. 6,	1966
20.0	**Flood Stage**	**20.20**	**Jan. 27,**	**1970**

—Data from National Weather Service – Medford, Oregon Office

earlier and in some streams, the flow was less. For Ashland, the trouble with Ashland Creek was similar as both floods, as well as the 1997 flood, took out the fresh water system and most of the forest access roads in the area. The Plaza gets flooded every time there is a major flood roaring down Ashland Canyon and politicians argue, after every flood, how to fix it. The January

Raging, muddy, flooding Bear Creek races under Barnett Road bridge in Medford. At peak of flood, water rose above the bank of the creek upstream only 200 yards, inundated the Crest Imperial Estates trailer park off Ellendale Drive and flooded low area west of the creek. The overflow from this low area put water over Barnett Street closing the street and the bridge for several hours. This view, by Preston Mitchell, was made from center of foot bridge a few feet downstream from Barnett Street Bridge.

1997 did less overall damage than the 1974 flood but the 1997 flood was very severe on Ashland's historical Plaza.

There is argument on what to do about floods. Some advocate building more and bigger dams. Dams hold flood water and did so very well in the New Year's Day 1997 flood. Another point is not to allow construction or trailer courts within known flood plains because nature will bring floods – "Act of God" – and a way to be prepared, is to keep the flood plains clear. ◇

Christmas Week Storm 1964
Heaviest Oregon rainfall December 1964 was at Illahe on the lower Rogue River: 41.43"
Five day heaviest rainfall total Illahe, Ore.   21.94"
Heaviest 24-hour rainfall Illahe, Ore.   8.23"
—Lucia. p. 72

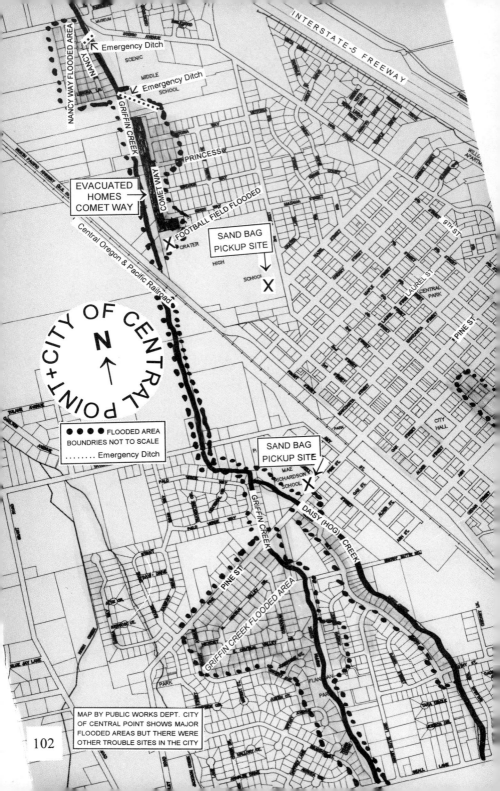

High Water in Central Point
Griffin Creek on a Rampage

If there is flooding at Ashland, and elsewhere in the so-called Upper Bear Creek Valley, the City of Central Point, which is about 20 miles down-stream from Ashland, has the potential of being flooded. Bear Creek, which skirts Central Point is at the city's eastern edge and receives all the waters from this entire watershed.

As far as anyone can recall, every time Ashland gets a flood so does Central Point. How badly Central Point gets wet varies on each occasion.

Bear Creek has not, in recent years, been of major concern in the city, but Griffin Creek, which bisects part of the town, must always be reckoned with.

Thanks to the National Weather Service and its heavy-rain and high-water forecast, Central Point's Public Works Department's people turned out in advance of the massive rainfall with heavy equipment and contracted with a construction company to wheel in more. In the days following the flood, some of the city workers took pictures of conditions and willingly loaned some of them to us.

Barbara Staus, and others who live on or near Comet Way, was one of the lucky ones. Griffin Creek invaded part of Crater High School's football field, residents' back yards, and Comet Way and Nancy Way became roaring rivers. At Barbara's home, the water seeped only to about six-inches deep in her garage. But next door it ran under a house and ruined all the non-rigid furnace ductwork. Down the street, Jeff Saltmarsh hastily posted a hand-lettered sign on his front yard tree reading:

FOR SALE - RIVER FRONTAGE

Both Barbara and Jeff loaned some of their newly made but now keepsake pictures of their experiences with the New Year's Day 1997 flood for this book.

Jack and Kathy Fowler live on Princess Way, just one door from the soon-to-be-flooded Comet Way. Due to constant rain late in December, they were aware of rising water on Thorn Oak

Jack and Kathy Fowler's home is second from corner of Princess and Comet Ways (TOP) at sand bags. —author photo. The sand bags (LOWER) saved their house on New Year's Day. —Courtesy: Jack and Kathy Fowler

Daisy Creek and Griffin Creeks come together near Richardson School. The overflowing creeks left their marks in the athletic field. —Courtesy: City of Central Point

in West Medford so Jack set out, at Kathy's insistence, to find some sand bags. He located some and then a city truck, while making rounds, brought more. By December 31st they had them filled and in place at the edge of their front yard.

It occurs that early in the year Jack refinanced their house and the new insurance company insisted on his buying flood insurance. He resisted, "vigorously," saying he was aware that Griffin Creek had, in years past, covered some lower-lying lawns and trickled down Comet Way, but his place was higher. Nevertheless, he lost the discussion and forked over nearly $400 extra for the flood insurance. Did he need the insurance during the New Year's Day 1997 flood?

The rising water from Griffin Creek was stopped by his sand bags about twenty feet from his front door. Kathy sighed, nervously shook her head and murmured, "We were fortunate." Jack declared, "We lucked out."

(TOP) **Kathy Fowler stands, after dawn on January 1, in nearly knee-deep flood at Princess and Comet Ways.** (INSET) **Jack Fowler, reinforced with a cup of coffee, after being up all night, steadies himself in knee deep water.** (LOWER) **"Comet River" looking north.**
—Courtesy: Jack and Kathy Fowler

Every house on west side of Comet Way was surrounded by flooding Griffin Creek
—Courtesy: Jack and Kathy Fowler

Only these dogs had fun because of the flood.
—Courtesy: Jack and Kathy Fowler

The City of Central Point was about as well prepared for a flood of this magnitude as could be expected. A policy at Public Works is to keep a supply of filled sand bags for immediate distribution, because there are seven creeks that flow through the town. When it looked like trouble, additional empty bags were sought to fill a quickly-forming need. (Eagle Hardware opened its loading dock on New Year's Day so a city truck could fetch 6,000 sand bags and, Grange Co-op had 500 bags which it delivered to the city shop.) City crews worked in shifts around the clock to assist citizens in filling and distributing the sand bags as well as placing high water warning barriers, cleaning plugged storm drains and improving discharge channels to help drain flood water. Trying to keep plugged storm drains clear was a major task. As the flood increased, drains re-plugged easily with the mud that the flood waters carried.

Public Works divided the city into five "battle" sectors and assigned a key person to each sector. Then another worker was

(TOP) **City crew dug emergency water escape channel with heavy equipment at north end of Comet Way to drain flood waters back into Griffin Creek beyond fence.** —Courtesy: Jeff Saltmarsh.

(LOWER) **One week later, water gone, channel remains. Pipes had been placed for this purpose only weeks earlier, but culvert proved much too small.** —author photo

assigned to coordinate communications and resources throughout the city. Due to the limited assets at the city's disposal and the enormity of the second flood – there were actually two floods with a short breather between – the crews were prioritized and worked under emergency conditions as trouble spots were reported. The major emphasis was to protect homes by providing sand bags to property owners and trying to keep the water drainages clear where possible.

Distribution locations for sand bags were set up at Crater High School and Mae Richardson Elementary as each is fairly close to the flooding Griffin Creek. Bags were also at the City Shop and handy for residents between 5th and 6th Streets bounded by Oak and Ash Streets, a low area, where about a dozen homes were saved by sand bagging. The site at the high school was closed after the first day.

Elk Creek, small enough to go unnoticed by its neighbors most of the time, had its own spree of flooding and sand bags saved a number of houses on White Chapel Drive.

"That Puny Creek"

A resident who recently moved into the neighborhood observed, "How wild that puny creek became in such a short time. I am amazed to the tune of thousands of dollars for repairs, and gross inconvenience, but luckily I have flood insurance and the community is lucky that nobody got hurt."

As closely as could be determined, the City of Central Point distributed about 29,000 sand bags in a 48-hour period starting Monday, December 30 at about 10 p.m.

There are seven creeks running through the city. Of these, six flooded. In the order of the worst flooding to the least are:

1. Griffin Creek
2. Jackson Creek
3. Daisy (Hog) Creek
4. Horn Creek
5. Elk Creek
6. Mingus Creek

Griffin Creek, which gets its start near Anderson Butte (elevation 5,195 feet) in the Siskiyou Mountains, was aggressive along most of its length. Southwest of Medford, at about 2,000

Nancy Way and Comet Way, a few blocks apart, were both flooded by Griffin Creek. Nancy "River" as it was dubbed, was eventually drained when the city brought heavy equipment to break concrete sidewalk allowing the flood to drain into the creek only 20 feet away.

feet elevation, it threatened one culvert then took out another through private driveways in the 4900 block of Griffin Creek Road. The creek here is usually maybe three feet wide, but this washout left an eight-foot deep rut about 12 feet wide.

Griffin Creek enters Central Point at the south city limits at Beall Lane, wanders through a low area to the main arterial (Pine Street), then has its waters multiplied near Mae Richardson Elementary School where it is joined by Daisy (Hog) Creek.

Between Beall Lane and Pine Street, Griffin Creek's flooding put over 100 homes at risk but these were saved by extensive placement of sand bags. (Daisy Creek, considerably smaller, which runs roughly parallel, a few blocks east, put 36 homes at risk with its own flood. These houses were also saved by piles of sand bags.)

Griffin Creek skirts downtown Central Point. The creek is supposed to be contained within a culvert when it reaches High-

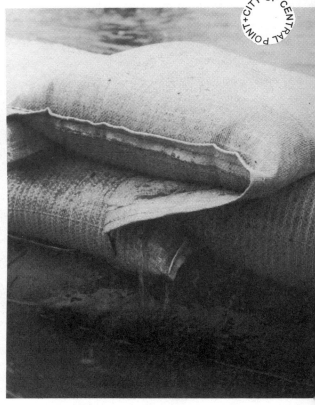

Sand bags today are made of fiberglass, cost at least 25¢ each. When full of dry sand bags weigh about 50 pounds. When wet, weight may be nearly double. Volunteers don't seem to realize the weight in the stress of moving full bags to save a house, but when it's time to empty the bags, ambition seems mostly gone.
—Courtesy: Jack and Kathy Fowler

way 99, but its waters put the railroad, parallel to the road, at risk and flowed over the highway to attack the track and football field at Crater High School. For about a quarter-mile along the creek, mud and water oozed between every house and filled Comet Way. With water on all sides of all the homes it was time to leave. The flood forced a general evacuation order for the occupants of 13 residences plus two more at the corner of Kings Way. Nine homes nearest the north end of Comet, where the flood water was the deepest, were saved by use of sand bags.

As the surge swamped Comet Way, a new water escape channel connecting the north end of Comet, adjacent to Scenic Middle School, where an area of its track had been covered with water and mud, with Griffin Creek was dug by Public Works. This relief ditch was about six feet wide and about three feet deep. The fact that the city crew was prompt with this project, contributed to lowering the water levels that were accumulating

Sand bags. Lots of them, saved this home.

late-colored Griffin Creek. Shouts went from house-to-house as the water deepened until it seems that everyone in the neighborhood, who was home, turned out with a common goal: save the houses. The city brought more and more sand bags, which were filled by even passersby. In the excitement of the night – still pouring down rain – property owners promptly dubbed the street "Nancy River."

The city brought in heavy equipment which broke then opened a 12-feet wide channel through a thick concrete sidewalk near the corner of Nancy and Scenic Avenue. The flood took to this sudden outlet and spewed itself across a twenty-foot wide slope back into the Griffin Creek channel near the front of the Crater Rock Museum. The museum, higher, was not damaged.

It doesn't make any difference as to the type of emergency taking place, non-usual occurrences attract crowds. Call the people "on-lookers," "spectators," "by-standers," "witnesses," "gawkers," "viewers," "observers," "watchers," etc., these folks, without exception, get in the way of essential workers, delivery

(TOP) **Water depth in houses on Comet Way varied from house-to-house. Barbara Staus points to water line on her home.** (LOWER) **Streets in western Central Point, Vincent Ave. and vicinity, inundated by flooding Griffin Creek, left much mess, mud everywhere. Truck load of sodden belongings being readied for trip to dump.**

(TOP) **Jeff Saltmarsh, who lives in second house from right, made this picture of "Comet River" early New Year's Day morning.**
— Courtesy: Jeff Saltmarsh.

(LOWER) **Flooding of Daisy Creek near Scenic Avenue.**
— Courtesy: City of Central Point

A fellow on Nancy Way said of the sand bag lines, "It's like building a fort with the enemy, the flood, on one side as we on the other."

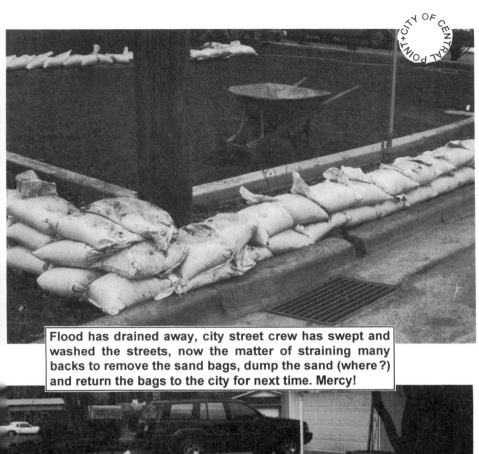

Flood has drained away, city street crew has swept and washed the streets, now the matter of straining many backs to remove the sand bags, dump the sand (where?) and return the bags to the city for next time. Mercy!

Weekend chore: Dump sand bags.

supply trucks and emergency vehicles. And so it was in the middle of the night, in heavy rain, when the flood was cresting. The police already had its hands full with normal New Year's Eve celebrants, the flood, and now crowd control. Even so, in the hardest hit areas, city personnel went door-to-door to offer assistance.

–0–

As we have seen, Central Point lies near the bottom end of the Bear Creek watershed and the town receives waters from the entire watershed when flooding occurs. Accordingly, it is not unreasonable to presume that Central Point could experience even greater damage in future floods. Within its means, the city is alert to its responsibilities. Some of the steps for being ready are:

    Update the city-wide Emergency Action Plan
    Enlarge bridge and culverts that proved too small
    Educate the public in flood prevention and flood protection
    Be certain that all storm drains are kept clear
    Rebuild its ready supply of filled sand bags
    Become aggressive in enforcing the city flood
       protection code.

It's all called being prepared. Central Point will be ready.◇

Blackwell Road, near Antelope Road, frequently goes under water in winter storms, but the New Year's Day flooding of nearby Bear Creek kept the road closed for days. Table Rock in background.
— Courtesy Jack and Kathy Fowler

Some Other Areas Troubled by Flood

In the Introduction of this book, we acknowledged that there were many areas throughout Oregon where the daily routine of life was interrupted by the flood of December 1996 - January 1997. The major scope of this book is the Bear Creek drainage in Jackson County, where we have seen the damage and turmoil primarily in Ashland and in Central Point. Talent, next door to Ashland, then Phoenix, four more miles to the north (down stream), and Medford, which is between Phoenix and Central Point have been included. But there was flood damage in many other places, far more than can be reported here.

We will let the pictures tell some of the other stories.

Seeping Rainwater

In many areas there are often low places in people's yards which, in a thunderstorm, leave pools of water which generally soaks into the earth in a short time. However, during the constant rain that fell in the days just before the New Year's Day flood, the pools deepened as the rain did not let up. For example, at Bob Hoolko's place on Griffin Creek Road, the raging creek was not his concern except for his driveway over a culvert, which held, but the voluntary back yard pool appeared. (His place is about 400 feet elevation above the creek). When seepage was observed in the basement, his wife, Anne, took a shovel and did some channeling at the pool while he rigged a small pump to start draining it.

Downhill aways, at Griffin Creek Elementary School, it was drainage from the rain, rather than the creek, that did the damage.

Lucky day: School library books escape damage.

Several classrooms had wet floors (easily dried) but in the school media center, which is on a lower floor plan, close to four inches of water accumulated. Luckily, the lowest book shelves were still several inches above water so no books were lost. But the fairly new carpet was a sopping mess and had to be pulled up.

Upper Griffin Creek, normally just a trickle, tore out private driveway culverts, bridges.

Flooded Bear Creek just south of Medford's Barnett Road exit ramp. On the other side of the trees lies Crest Imperial Estates, a mobile home park that was inundated. (See pictures pages 82, 83, 84.) —Courtesy: Yvonne Rowe

Lynn Newbry County Park, which had been developed by much volunteer labor, was totally wrecked by flooding Bear Creek.

123

Bear Creek Kiwanis Club, which had a hand in Newbry park's creation, must muster many men and women to restore the park. Funding, if any, awaits government decisions.

(TOP) **Forest Creek, west of Jacksonville, took out a bridge shown here in remnants.** (LOWER) **Forest Creek over-ran its culverts on Forest Creek Road, tied up traffic.** —Courtesy: Marguerite Black

The Red Lion Motel on Medford's Riverside Avenue, looks out on often stagnant Bear Creek, the still water caused by an irrigation district dam, soon to be re-moved, a few blocks downstream. But the New Year's Day 1997 flood saw waters angrily lapping almost at guests' doors.

—Courtesy: Gary Breeden

A "cutaway" is a term defining pictures not directly involved with the main topic but having a side-interest to the subject.

(TOP) Street vagrant holds sign in Medford's Bear Creek Plaza adjacent to McDonald's restaurant reading:

HOMELESS / OUT OF WORK / FLOODED OUT

Passersby have amply provided bags of food at his feet.

(LOWER) Early morning temperatures in the days following the flood were below freezing. This orchard heater (smudge pot) was near the garage of the Talent Water District.

(OPPOSITE PAGE AND THIS PAGE) **Several reasonably new houses on Joseph St., Talent, were endangered when Wagner Creek cut a new channel. The dwelling at 265 Joseph tipped over after the ground beneath it washed away.**

Larson Creek

Most of the Rogue Valley's creeks "don't amount to much," said a Realtor, but come flood time, think again! Larson Creek, that runs in southeast Medford, left its banks on New year's Day 1997. See pictures on pages 130, 131, 132. The creek, usually within its channel (LOWER), went over Ellendale Drive (TOP) and flooded field south of the creek. Lower picture looks east from Gary Breeden's architect office. —Courtesy: Gary Breeden

Larson Creek

The creek looking west toward Gary Breeden's building at flood stage (TOP)
—Courtesy: Gary Breeden **One week later** (LOWER)
—author.

Larson Creek

Larson Creek (TOP) did not damage Larson Creek Retirement Center at 1025 Ellendale Drive but over-ran its north bank and flooded a number of the 82 units at the low-income Barnett Road Townhouse family complex (background). —Courtesy: Ruth Watson. (LOWER) Cheryl Breeden, wife of architect Gary Breeden, smiles with relief that their building escaped damage. Barnett Townhouses to left, rear, Larson Creek Retirement Center, right, rear.
—Courtesy: Gary Breeden

Covering the New Year's Day 1997 Flood
Newspapers and Television

One of the most fragile things in the world is "news." When something thought to be newsworthy gets into the wind, it is said the story is "breaking" so reporters and photographers head for the scene. In non-print technology, when a television station "breaks" into a program with a news bulletin, the announcer proclaims the story to be "breaking." After the story hits the newspaper front pages, or is the first story of the programmed news cast, it is said the story has "broken." Next comes follow-up then conclusions – if indeed there is any follow-up.

In the old days, schedules in the newspaper business were based on the hour and minute a paper hit the street. These schedules were very firm – engraved in granite – because publishers depended on almost split-minute timing when it came to delivering bundles of papers to trains and buses which ran on published schedules. If one of these departures was missed because the paper was late, and the competing newspaper was on time, sales were lost, complaints poured in and major chaos occurred in the editor's and circulation manager's offices – and sometimes heads rolled.

In earlier years, as recent as the 1940's, the majority of newspaper sales were on street corners. To keep schedules firm in the press rooms in the face of a breaking story, such as a bad fire, impending flood, maybe a railroad wreck, a teaser paragraph or two was inserted on the front page and the papers were rushed to the streets. As the event developed with reporters and photographers on the scenes, the presses rolled "EXTRA" editions which were rushed to the key street corners where street sales vendors actually screamed the headlines at the passersby.

People gobbled the papers, which sold from 2¢ or 3¢ to a nickel a copy, as fast as the papers became available. The people learned about what was happening in depth by reading the newspapers.

Radio news got a start in 1919 but it was several years before there were enough listeners to cause the papers any competition. In fact, many early radio stations were owned by and

Libby Dowsett, KOBI-NBC TV-5 reporter, on the job reporting damage at Bear Lake Mobile Estates.

operated from the editorial rooms of newspapers.

> In Medford, Oregon, The *Mail Tribune* did regular scheduled news casts from its studio in the newspaper building over KYJC (AM-radio) from the 1950's extending to 1973. Al Reiss, a *Mail Tribune* reporter, who was one of the newscasters, recalled that during the 1972 flood, KYJC had a mobile transmitter that went from place-to-place during special events – floods, fires, election night – for remote broadcasts.

Those who depended on home delivery found the paper on schedule daily between about 4 and 5:30 p.m., but the home edition often missed the excitement of the breaking story and rare it was when an "EXTRA – hot off the press" was fed to the home routes. For the public, radio took up the slack.

So-called daily "afternoon" newspapers regularly published from three to six editions between about 11 a.m. and 6 p.m. But the number of editions on a single day could easily jump to 10 or more if the story was hot enough. These were the days when many news editors were cigar-chompers, swilled black coffee, were sometimes profane, and grew ulcers in an effort to be first on the street with the news and above all else, "keep to the schedule."

During the Ashland New Year's Day 1997 flood, the Medford *Mail Tribune* and the *Ashland Daily Tidings* kept to their regular schedules regardless of the status of the breaking story of the flood. Each town is a "single-newspaper" town – no printed competition, street sales are minor, therefore no incentive to publish "EXTRA" editions. Each paper did its one edition a day. About 20 percent of the press run goes to street sales (mostly coin machines) and about 80 percent routine home delivery.*

Television news people were at the Ashland flood just as quickly as were newspaper reporters (both keep police scanners in their offices), but the broadcast people had an advantage over the press: Instant broadcast – often from the scene directly into the airwaves and into people's TVs or radios if the station managers want to do so.

Retrievability !

The printed media, a newspaper, is the key to "retrievability." Days or weeks or years afterward, when one needs to go back and study the New Year's Day 1997 Flood, the newspaper is retrievable. Hard copies are usually kept in the editorial offices for awhile, and micro-film of the papers is available in public libraries and elsewhere.

Television coverage of a flood, as an example, is exciting to look at. Moving pictures of the swirling water, houses, automo-

---

* Data from *Mail Tribune*. The *Mail Tribune*, being a morning paper, is released to routes about 1 a.m. for daily delivery by 6:30 a.m. (Weekend numbers and schedules are different.) If a hot story "breaks" after about midnight, by the time the paper prints it the item is 24-hours old and the TV people have "scooped" the newspaper. By the time the next paper is ready, the story has grown stale.

biles, barns, whatever, are being wrecked or carried away – Red Cross Disaster teams at work – but television and radio news is all gone in a split second. It is not generally retrievable.

For the New Year's Day 1997 Flood in Southern Oregon, the three regional newspapers, Medford *Mail Tribune*, the Grants Pass *Courier* and the *Ashland Daily Tidings*, as well as the three network-affiliated television stations, KDRV-12 (ABC), KOBY-5 (NBC) and KTVL-10 (CBS), together kept everyone who wanted to know what was going on informed in a superior manner.

The *Ashland Daily Tidings* ran front page stories about the flood for 14 consecutive issues. A special insert about the flood appeared on January 7.

The Medford *Mail Tribune* ran front page stories about the flood for 13 consecutive issues. A special insert about the flood appeared on January 9. A comprehensive list of articles for further reading about the New year's Day 1997 flood is in the bibliography of this book.

Three Medford television stations and the Ashland Cable-TV station offered (for sale) special 30-minute video tapes containing some of their flood coverage. ◇

"30"

Appendix
The Red Cross, A Brief History

The International Red Cross movement was started in Switzerland in 1863, then, after the sessions of a body of delegates representing 16 governments of Europe in 1864, with an American non-voting delegate (Charles S. Bowles, of the U.S. Sanitary Commission) observing, found that a volunteer relief organization could work effectively with the various governments in time of war.

The idea for such an organization was in the mind of Henry Dunant who wrote a book, *A Memory of Solferino,* published in 1862. His book was an appeal against the terrifying inhumanity he had seen after the Battle of Solferino which left 40,000 dead and wounded on the field. Dunant, a salesman, sent his coach into town to obtain relief supplies then he sought aid from his friends to help the wounded. That would have been the end of it except that he wrote the book. Its closing pages offered proposals that became the germ for the Red Cross movement.

His emphasis was for trained volunteers and the necessity for international cooperation for the sake of humanity. He proposed that "societies" be formed in the various countries for relief work. The symbol, a red cross on a white background, was adopted and first worn as an armband by a physician in the field during the Prussian-Danish War of 1864.

Clarissa Harlowe Barton later known just as Clara Barton, founded what became the Red Cross in the United States in 1861. This was when she, and some women friends, attended the needs of some wounded and some hungry soldiers who arrived in Washington, D.C. Her work was on behalf of such groups as the U. S. Sanitary Commission. She often collected needed articles then personally gave them to the victims of the war, then she learned how to store supplies and set up distribution methods. But her work was more than just handing out needed items. She often sat with wounded men, wrote letters for them, listened to their troubles and prayed with them.

In 1869, when she was in Switzerland, friends introduced her to the Red Cross idea. Afterward, she promoted the thought of the United States joining with the other nations in the international association.

Clara Barton, and some of her supporters, formed the American Association of the Red Cross as a District of Columbia corporation in 1881. By Act of Congress in March 1882, the organization was officially recognized. President Chester A. Arthur, President of the United States, signed a Proclamation on July 26, 1882 that notified the people of the nation of the adherence to a treaty and acceptance of that ratification between the United States of America and the Swiss Confederation.

In 1893, the American National Red Cross was created by re-incorporation and was given charters by Congress in 1900 then again in 1905. This charter with its amendments became a basis for today's American Red Cross.

Today's organization is devoted largely to disaster relief which Miss Barton introduced to many other national societies. The Red Cross relies mostly on volunteers for its workers.

The U. S. Post Office recognized Clara Barton with a special commemorative 3¢ stamp issued on September 7, 1948. Another commemorative stamp (5¢) recognizing the International Red Cross was called the "Red Cross Centenary Issue" stamp of October 29, 1963. On June 29, 1995, a 32¢ postage stamp featuring Clara Barton was issued as part of a Civil War set. <>

The Salvation Army, A Brief History

The Salvation Army started in England in 1865 when William Booth, a Methodist minister, left his church to start Christian Mission Centers in the London slums. He adopted the name, "Salvation Army" in 1878, and organized as a military-like group with "Corps," "Commissioned Officers" (ordained clergy), and "soldiers" (members of his congregations).

Organized church groups didn't like his methods because his methods were "unconventional." The Salvation Army did not meet in church buildings but offered worship services in less formal settings as tents, dance halls, and the like. In addition to its evangelical services, the Army successfully attacked social ills by feeding the hungry, offering beds to the homeless and offering hope to the impoverished.

Booth's book, *In Darkest England and the Way Out,* set a pattern for social welfare. The work with his "Army" was totally without government money or sanction.

Seven young women, directed by Commissioner George Scott Railton, set up a small headquarters in New York City in 1880. Here they combined street corner religious services and an hymn playing Salvation Army brass band (the band caught the attention of passersby to note that something was happening), with feeding the poor.

By the early 1900's, the organization was well underway with a program they had started in 1884 for woman's social concerns. By 1888 this "Army" was operating a food bank, then started a daycare center in 1890. In 1901 it opened the first Salvation Army missionary hospital.

During World War II, the Salvation Army had about 3,000 field service units for the benefit of the armed forces of the Allies. In addition to a traditional letter writing service and field chaplain help, this "Army" (as well as the Red Cross) provided donuts and coffee to another "army" – the soldiers who were packing rifles and often trying to sleep in muddy foxholes.

The Salvation Army led in the formation of the United Service Organization (USO) that had responsibility for morale building by providing entertainment in the field.

The Salvation Army has always been an international charitable and religious movement. It helps all people in need regardless of age, color, race, creed or sex. It offers food, clothing, shelter in the face of disaster and in the aftermath of disaster as well as on a day-to-day basis. Members work to promote spiritual, moral and physical well being with many sponsorships some of which are:

    Medical clinics   Missing persons bureau
    Hospitals   Summer camps
    Children's homes   Boy's clubs
    Foster care   Men's social service centers
    Skid road centers   Day care centers
    Homes for senior citizens Employment Service
          Evangeline Residences for Business Women
        Special maternity hospitals for unmarried women

During the Christmas season, the Salvation Army, with its street corner Red Kettle and other special programs, provides food and clothing and seasonal remembrances to over 2,000,000 forgotten people.

While the Coast Guard sports the motto *Semper Paratus* ("Always Ready"), the Salvation Army is also "Always Ready" in times of disaster with its mobile canteens (food wagons), free clothing, furniture, blankets, medical supplies as well as a meaningful spiritual ministry.

The Salvation Army was recognized by the U. S. Post Office Department when on July 2, 1965, there was a commemorative 5¢ stamp issued for the centenary of the founding of the organization. ◇

Bert and Margie Webber, with "world's largest coffee cup."(See page 76.)

About the Authors

Bert and Margie Webber have been writing and publishing books about the Oregon Country for a number of years. When a spot-news story, as the New Year's Day 1997 flood swept through Ashland and their own town of Central Point a few miles away, Bert's former newspaper reporting prowess surfaced with the desire to do a book about the flood. Timeliness was important so other projects were put aside and the two went "full bore" on the flood topic.

Bert holds a degree in journalism from Whitworth College in Spokane, Washington. He is also a librarian having earned the Master of Library Science degree from studies at Portland State University and the University of Portland. He has written well over one hundred newspaper and periodical features and spot news articles as well as, with his wife's assistance, over fifty non-fiction books.

Margie holds a Bachelor of Science degree in nursing from the University of Washington and has done post-graduate work. She served in many different nursing positions, including school nursing and public health. For the books, she serves as an editor, a telephone communicator and often as a field photographer.

The Webbers live in Central Point, just west of the flood plain of Bear Creek, and east of the plain of the fitful Griffin Creek. ◇

Bibliography and Reading List

> The newspaper section of this bibliography serves as a source list for this book. It is also a guide for additional matter from the papers about the flood for researchers. The newspapers are listed by name, then chronologically, and cover from January 2 through January 31, 1997. They will likely be available on microfilm in libraries in Ashland, Medford, University of Oregon, Southern Oregon State College and at the Oregon State Library. — Editor

BOOKS

Barton, Clara. *The Red Cross, A History*.... Private Print. 1898.

Geographic Names System (Oregon). Branch of Geographic Names, U. S. Geological Survey [unfinished] Dec. 1992.

Gilbo, Patrick F. *The American Red Cross*. Harper. 1981.

Lucia, Ellis. *Wild Water; The Story of the Far West's Great Christmas Week Floods*. Private print. 1965.

Maddox, Wal. *The Flood of Christmas Week 1964* [at Rogue River, Ore.]. Private print. [1965].

From the Mountains to the Sea; Flood and Disaster; Southern Oregon - Northern California; Hell from High water; The People and Their Courage. Private print. nd [1965].

O'Hara, Marjorie. *Ashland, the First 130 Years*. Private Print. 1986.

"Rogue River Basin" in *Postflood Report - December 1964 - January 1965 FLOOD*. Portland District, U.S. Army Corps of Engineers. 1966. pp. 145-168.

"What You Should Know About The Salvation Army." Bete, Inc. So.Deerfield, MA. 1990 Ed.

NEWSPAPERS

Ashland Daily Tidings (Ashland, Oregon)

"Don't Drink the Water." Jan. 2. p.1.

"Mud, Water Invade Ashland Homes, Businesses." Jan. 2. p.1.

"Portable Toilets, Bottled Water are all the Rage as Residents Settle in for Stint Without Water." Jan. 3, 1997. p.1.

"I-5 Closure, Leave Thousands Stuck in Ashland." Jan. 3, 1997. p.2.

"Living Without Water Can be an Adventure." Jan. 3, 1997. p.5.

"Governor Tours Flood's Devastation." Jan. 4, 1997. p.1.

"First Baby Delivered Safe From Flood." Jan. 4, 1997. p.3.

"Goodwill Abundant in Hard Times." Jan. 4,1997. p.5.

"Ashland Churches Escape Flood Damage, Pitch in to Help Others.' Jan. 4. p.6.
"Hot Springs Emerges From Mud." Jan. 6, 1997. p. 5.
"Elderly Couple Glad Someone Saw the Light." Jan. 7. p.3.
"The End is Near." Jan 7. p.4.
"We're Closer Than we Ever Wanted; Our Shared Crisis is Making "Friends Out of People Who do Nothing More Than Squat Together." Jan. 7. p.4.
"City Sustains $4.5 Million in Damage." Jan. 9. p.1.
"Apartment Complex Merges from Mire." Jan. 9. p. 2.
"Park's Main Entrance, Playground Closed." Jan. 9. p. 3.
"Talent Water System Barely Hanging On." Jan. 9. p.3
"Go Ahead and Drink the Water." Jan. 11, 1997. p.1.
"Plaza Searches For Business as Usual." Jan. 13. p.3.
"Move, Sell or Rebuild; Talent Darken Subdivision Owners Debate What to do with Their Condemned Home. Jan. 14. p.1.
"Flooded-Out Seniors Look for New Homes. Jan. 15. p.1
"Big Floods: Mother nature Flexing Her Muscles." Jan. 15. p.6.
"Culvert, Winburn Repairs May Take Until Spring." Jan. 16. p.2.
"Talent Residents Ponder Creek's Behavior." Jan. 16. p.3.
"Homeowners Eligible For Up to $200,000 in Loans For Flood Damage." Jan. 17. p.3.
"[Senator] Wyden Vows Push For Federal Flood Aid For Ashland." Jan. 17. p.2.
"[National] Guard: It's Our Job to Help; Local Guardsmen Regroup After Two Weeks of Flood Work." Jan. 18. p.1.
"Council Considers Loan Plan for Plaza Shops." Jan. 18. p.1.
"SBA Loans Aid Flooded Businesses, Homes." Jan 18. p.8
"Talent Water Back Monday; Ashland Lifts Conservation." Jan. 18. p.1.
"Historical Society Offers Tip For Saving Flooded Mementos." Jan. 18. p. 5.
"One-Third of Plaza Open." Jan. 21. p.3.
"Flood Relief Funds Abound in Local Businesses, Banks." Jan. 21. p.3.
"It's Official: We're A Disaster." Jan. 24. p.1.
"Flood Leaves Greenway in Pieces." Jan. 24. p.2.
"Here's When Being a Disaster Area is a Good Thing. " Jan 24. p.4.
"City Won't Need to Borrow all of $2.6 Million Bond." Jan. 25. p.1.
"Watershed Partnership Hopes to Influence Ashland's Flood Repair." Jan. 25. p.4
"Talent Water Fully Restored." Jan. 27. p.1.
"FEMA Views Bear Lake [Mobile Estates] Damage." Jan. 30. p.1.
"Ashland's Intertie [with Medford Water System] cost: $1 Million." Jan. 30. p.2.

"Flood Forecasting Should Get Better." Jan. 30. p.6
"FEMA, SBA Offer Flood-relief Guidelines to Residents." Jan. 31. p.3.

Central Valley Times (Grants Pass, Oregon)
"Streams Have Too Much to Drink on New Year's" Jan. 8, 1997.p. 1A.
"[Senator] Wyden Pressing For Disaster Designation." Jan. 22. p.1.

Mail Tribune (Medford, Oregon)
"Wet and Wild; Flooding Takes Out Homes and Roads. Jan. 2, 1997. p.1A.
"Floodwaters Swamp Ashland." Jan. 2, 1997. p.1A.
"Mobile Homes Hit Hard by Flooding." Jan 2, 1997. p.1A, 12A.
"Water Everywhere: Not A Drop to Drink." Jan 2, 1997. p. 4A
"Safe But Soggy; Damages Extensive in Ashland, Elsewhere." Jan. 3. p.1A.
"Phoenix, Talent Roll With Bear Creek's Punch." Jan. 3. p.2A.
"Rescuers Save 2 in Plaza" Jan 3. p.6A
"After the Flood: Digging Out; Home Was Hard-Hit but They Still Love the River." Jan. 3. p.1.
"Applegate Knocks Out Power; River Residents Avert Serious Damage." Jan 3. p.2.
"Corps' Dam Strategy Kept Flows Down." Jan. 3. p.2.
"Water Emergency Won't Be Over Quickly." Jan. 3, p.5A.
"Kitzhaber Gets Post-Deluge Tour." Jan. 4. p.1A
"Oh, What A Mess There Is; Cleanup Will Take Time, Cost a Bundle." Jan 4. p.1A.
"Porta-Potties: The Insult After Injury." Jan. 4. p.1C
"Be Safe. test Your Well Water." Jan. 5. p.1A.
"Floodwaters Level Lithia Park; Plaza Business Owners Get a Look." Jan 5. p.1B
"Survived the flood? Don't Fall For a Scam." Jan. 5. p.1B
"After the Floods, the T-Shirt Sales Began." Jan. 5. p.3B.
"Ashland Eateries Go Extra Mile; Water Tanks, Pumps Keep Food Coming." Jan. 6. p.2A.
"Red Cross Meals Feed Flood Victims." Jan.7. p.1A
"Many Hands Help Hospital Stay Open." Jan 7. p.3A
"After the Flood - Before the Recriminations, Be Thankful For What Survived." Jan. 7. p.8A.
"Red Cross Offers Help, Hope; Flood Victims Pack Center in Medford." Jan 8. p.1A
"Park Swan Squashed By Truck." Jan. 8. p.3A.
"State to Issue Emergency Permits to Landowners With Streamside Erosion." Jan. 8. p.3A.
"Medford, C[entral] P[oint] Schools Also Had Damage." Jan.9. p.3A.

"Flood Damage Costly; County Estimates $44 Million." Jan. 10. p.1A.
"Ashland Council To Float Bond Issue; Ashland Flood Damage Estimates." Jan. 10. p.2A.
"Pay Up, Elk Creek Critics." Jan. 10. p.10A
"Anatomy of a Flood." Jan. 12. p.1A-2A
"Flood's Trauma Could Increase Drug Problems." Jan. 13. p.3A
"Flooding Tally Tops $50 Million; FEMA, State Teams Evaluate Damage." Jan. 14. p.1A.
"Completed Elk Creek Dam Would Have Helped in Flood." Jan. 17. p.3A.
"A Tragedy Just Waiting to Happen; Flooding Takes Big Toll on Mobile Homes Near Creeks." Jan. 19. p.1A.
"[Gov.] Kitzhaber Makes Formal Aid Request; Clinton Asked For Disaster Declaration. Jan. 19. p.1B.
"Reviewing the Lessons; Ashland Apparently Has Still More to Learn About Flooding." Jan. 26. p 1B, 5B.
"FEMA Team Will Visit to Work on Flood Aid; Types of Flood Damage Relief Vary." Jan. 30. p.3A.
"Flood Rings Miners' Gold Bell; High Water Stirs Dreams of Nuggets." Jan. 31. p.1A.
"Settle Water Questions Before You Buy Home; Seller Must Disclose Flood Plain Information." Jan. 31. p.3A.
"When, Not If; 1861, 1890, 1927, 1948, 1974, 1997 Floods Are An Ashland Reality." Jan. 31. p.8A.
"Rogue Gorge Renewed; Jan. 1 Flood Removes Decades of Debris." Jan. 31. p.1B, 3B.

The Oregonian (Portland)

"Floodwaters Stage Ashland Drama; Worried About Contamination, Officials in Ashland Turn Off the City's Water System." Jan. 5. p.A1.
"Ashland Flooding Eases; Officials Checking Damage in the Aftermath of the High water." Jan. 4. p.A1.
"Flooding: Pack Mules Haul Supplies.: Jan. 4. p.A9
"Ashland Residents Turn Effort to Salvage." Jan. 5. p.A1.
"Ashland Mobile Homes Damaged Beyond Repair." Jan. 5. p.A16.

Index

Page numbers in ***bold italic*** type are pictures and maps

American Red Cross, *see*: Red Cross
Anderson Butte, 110
Angus Bowmer Theater, *24*
Ashlander Apartments (flooded), 31
Ashland City Hall, *14*, 22
Ashland Community Club, 23
Ashland Community Hospital, 32, 77; water for, 77
Ashland Creek Watershed, *x*
Ashland Creek, *back cover, 11, 14;* 15; flood, *42*, 43, 44, 100; (map), *12, 13,*
Ashland Creek, at Callé Guanajuato, *53*
Ashland Daily Tidings, *see*: newspapers
Ashland Fire Department, 36
Ashland flood, as photo opportunity, 30
Ashland Fudge Company (flooded), *47, 68*
Ashland Masonic Bldg. (map), *13*
Ashland mayor, 18
Ashland Plaza, 31; considered dangerous, 18; (flooded), *iii, vi, 14, 24, 47, 69,* (map), *13*
Ashland Police Dept., 18, *20,* 22, *58*
Ashland Sewer treatment plant, 16
Ashland water system. 16
Ashland, as resilient city, 48
Ashland, elev., 16
Ashland, flooded, 25
Ashland, Main Street, flooded, *69*
Ashlander Apartments, flooded, 41, 43
Astell, Marne, 30

Astell, Marne, 30
Bank of America, 37n
banks, loans, 36-37
Barnett Road Townhouse family complex, 67, *132*
Barnett Road/Bridge, *101*
Barton, Clara, 137-138
Bear Creek Greenway - Bike Trail, *91*
Bear Creek Kiwanis Club, *124*
Bear Creek pumping station, 43-44
Bear Creek Watershed (upper), *ix*
Bear Creek, flood, 19
Bear Creek, floods, 16, *50*
Bear Creek, origin of, 79n
Bear Lake Mobile Estates, 66; flooded, *80, 81, 85*
Beau Club Cocktails, privies at, *72*
bibliography, 17m
Black, Marguerite (photog), 125
Bloomsbury Books (store), 36
Bluebird Park, damage, 43, 45, 71
Boalister, Rick, quoted, 63
Bonneville Power Adm., 45
Boy Scouts, 26
Breeden, Cheryl, *132*
Breeden, Gary, architect, 130, 132; as photog., 130, 131, 132
Brown, Paula, 43-44
Burroughs, Karin, *34*
Butler Band Shell, 43; (map), *12, 13*
Butler Creek, 51

Callé Guanajuato, *11, 14, 52, 53, 54, 85*
Cannon, Hollie, 78-79
Caster, Nanci, 67
cellular phone, 51

146

Central Point Comet Way flooded, 103, *104, 106, 107, 108, 109, 111*
Central Point Nancy Way flooded, *111*
Central Point Public Works Dept., 103, 108, 110,112
Central Point Sch. Dist., 48
Central Point Vincent Avenue, 114
Central Point, Blackwell Road flooded, *119*
Central Point, flood prevention plans, 118
chemical toilets, 46, 63, *72, 73*
  etiquette for, 72-73; *Mail Tribune* quoted, 73; thanks for, 76
coffee, taste of, 23
condemned property, 45, *82, 84*
Cook, Jean, quoted, 46
Crater High School, 103, 112
Crater Rock Museum, 113
Crest Imperial Estates, 122, *82, 83, 84*
crowds, defined, 113
culverts, plugged, 45

Daisy Creek, *115*
Daisy Creek, floods, *105*
deaths, none, 59
dentist, *see:* Zundel, Dr. Rob't
Dowsett, Libby, TV reporter, *134*
Dritchas, Leanna, 30

Elizabethan Theater *24;* chemical toilets at, 74, *75;* (map), *12, 13*
Ellison, Kari. 30
Emigrant Creek,79n
Emigrant Dam. 16n
Emigrant Lake, 16n, 79n
4-wheel-drive vehicles, 26, 29
Falkenhagen, Mari, cook, *61*
Finnell, Dick, musician, 25-26

Firemen, 23
flood control, methods, 95-96
flood plain, 87
flooded out, what to do, 39
floods (local area - history), 97, 101
floods, 1964, *96*, 98, 99; 100; 1974, 97, 99, 100
Flower Tyme shop *v,* (flooded), *47*
food trucks," *see:* Red Cross Emergency Relief Vehicles
Forest Creek, floods, *125*
Fowler, Gloria (photog), iii, v, 22
Fowler, Jack, 30; -Kathy, 30
Fowler, Jack and Kathy (photogs), 104, 106, 107, 108, 112
Fowler, Jack and Kathy, house, **104;** quoted, 105
Fowler, Rod, 30
Frodsham, Hazel, 30
Frodsham, Joe, (photog), vi, 11, 14, 22, 24
Frodsham's Photofinishing Ashland plant, 30; Medford plant, 30

Golden, Cathy (mayor - Ashland), 18
Crest Imperial Estates, 82-84
Granite St. *14*, 15-16, *32*
Griffin Creek (floods), 48, 103-118
Griffin Creek (upper), *121*
Griffin Creek Elementary School library, flooded, *120*
Guanajuato Way, 23; (map), *12*; *see also*: Callé Guanajuato

Hamilton Creek (flooded),31, 41
Harris, Dean, quoted, 64
Highway 99 (flooded), 23, 41
Hill, Jason, 30
Hillah Shrine Temple, ***back cover***, 23, 31, *33*; *see also*: Shrine

147

Temple Holiday RV Park, flood damage, *92, 93*
Hosler, Earl R., 97; dam, 97
I.O.O.F. Bldg. (map), *13*
Information Desk (Ashland Police), 18, *20*
Internal Revenue Service, 36

Jackson Hot Springs, 25, 66; (flooded), *40*, 41; rescues at, 25
James, Sharon, experiences, 29
Johnson, Muriel, 44
Jorstad, Shelly, 30
Joseph, Linda and Tessah, *21*
Juniper Baptist Assn., *60*; field kitchen, *60*; volunteers, *60*

KOBI-TV, 51, *134*
Larson Creek floods, *130, 131, 132*
Larson Creek Retirement Center, *132*
Ledous, Kirsten, 41, 43
Lehburger, Gerry, 25
Lithia Artisans Market, *52*
Lithia Park, 15; (flooded), *11, 14*
Lithia Park damage, 23, off limits, 23; cause of, 45; dike built, 45; fire wood from, *43*
Lithia Park, inundated, 23, *24, 42*, 43
Lithia Park, swans in, *49*
Loren, R. (photog), 22, 47, 52, 69
Luman Road, flooded, *27*, 81

Main Street (Ashland), *24*
maps, Central Point, *102*
maps, Lithia Park (before flood), *12*; -(after flood), *13,* Rogue River Basin, *viii,* Ashland Creek, *x,* Upper Bear Creek, *ix*
McDonald's restaurant, *127*
McDowell, Dulcie, 30
McKie, Barbara, 25

Medford *Mail Tribune, 17,* 135, 136; broadcasts news 134
Medford, as water source, 34
Milner, Rachelle, 30
Mitchell, Preston (photog), 94, 101
mobile homes, at risk, 81-85
Morgan, Ben, quoted, 25
motels, 22
Mt. Ashland, elev. 16; Ski Area, 31
mud, at Ashland Plaza, 39; at Jackson Hot Springs, 25, *40,* 45, 47, *55;* mires cars, 26; slide, *32*
mud, Griffin Creek, 48
Munchies (restaurant), *55, 56*

National Guard Armory, as shelter, *62*
National Guard water service, 16, 23, 30-31, *34*, 38,
National Weather Service, 15, 84, 103
Nauvoo Trailer Park, *iv,* 16, 22-23; flooded, 66, *86, 87, 88, 89*; Red Cross food at, 88; water station at, *88*, wreckage, *86, 89*
Newbry Park, flooded, 123, 124
newspapers, 33, 45, 66, 73, 76, 133-136; *Ashland Daily Tidings,* 16; *17, 32,* 41, 46, 135, 136; quoted, 23; *Mail Tribune, 17, Central Valley Times, 17*
Niles, Mike, 30

Oregon RV Roundup trailer park, *90, 91*
Oregon State Employment Dept., 38-39
Owens, Dylan, born, 77
Owens, Micah and Lynette, 77
"Paula Pump," 44
Phillips, Dorothea, U S WEST, *93*

> **Photographers**
> Black, Marguerite, 125
> Breeden, Gary, 130, 131, 132
> Fowler, Gloria, iii, v, 22
> Fowler, Jack and Kathy, 104, 106, 107, 108, 112
> Frodsham, Joe, vi, 11, 14, 22, 24
> Loren, R., 22; 69
> Mitchell, Preston, 94, 101
> Rowe, Yvonne, 90, 122
> Saltmarsh, Jeff, 109, 115
> Webber, Bert, vi, 22
> Webber, Michael E., 40
> Zundel, Rob't and Laura, 27

Plaza businesses, *14, 24*; -flooded, *iii, v*; (map), *13*
Pope, Steven, 30
porta-potties, 73, *see also*: chemical toilets
postage stamps, *138, 140*
precautions, health/safety, 63, 64
pumps, *57*

Red Cross, services, 16-17
Red Cross chartered, 59, 138; Disaster Cleanup Kits, 59; Disaster Relief, 36-37; -Emergency Relief Vehicles, *iv, 58, 61*; -founded, 137, emergency shelters, 26, 59; meals served, 59; mops, *68;* on postage stamps, *138;*;
Red Lion Motel (Medford), *126*
Reeder Reservoir, 16, 97; no access, 45
Reiss, Al, reporter, 134
Renaissance Rose (store), *33*
restaurants, closed, *20, 55*
restaurants, open, 41
Richardson Elem. Sch., 111
Robinson, Vicki, 48
Roca Creek, floods, *50*
Rogue River Basin, (map), *viii*; Upper Bear Creek Watershed, *ix*; Ashland Creek Watershed, *x*

Rogue River, rages, *94*
Ross, Cal and Zoeann, rescued, 41
Rowe, Yvonne (photog), 90, 122

Safeway Store, 32; as chemical toilet site, *73, 74;* locations, 74
Saltmarsh, Jeff, photog, 109, 115
Salvation Army Thrift Store, Ashland, 65, 67; Medford, 66
Salvation Army, cleanup kits, 65; emergency services, 65, 68; founded, 139; Johnson, Mick, quoted, 65, 67; mission, 140; mobilized, 65; mops, *68;* on postage stamps, *140*
sand bag sites Central Point (map), *102*
sand bags, Ashland, *70*
sand bags, Central Point, distributed, 110; reserve, 108, sites, 110; specifications, 112
sand bags, in use, Central Point, *104, 107*, 112, 113, 116, 117, 118
sand bags, weight of, 22
Schmeling, Herman and Sylvia, reports damage, 50
schools, closed, 38, 41
Shakespeare Theaters, *24*
Shrine Band, 31
Shrine Temple, *11, 14, 24;* (map), *13*
Siskiyou Mountains, 16, 110
smudge pot (orchard heater), *127*
Southern Oregon Concert Band, 31
Southern Oregon State College, closed, 38, 41
Sparks, James, TV reporter, 51
Staus, Barbara, 103, *114*
swans, Lithia Park, *49*
swans, pool for, *24*

Talent Irrigation Dist., flow (chart), *78*; history of, 79n

Talent Water District, 127m
Talent water pump house, wrecked, *38*
Talent, water supply, 37-38
telephones, 46; damaged, *40;* repairs, 93
television cameraman swims, 51
television, 33, 36, 73, 76, 133-136
Thompson, Jackie, 30
trailers, in Oregon, 23; - in Jackson County, 23
trash, 47, *54, 70, 114*
Tree House Books, *iii*, 44
T-shirts, *37*
U S WEST, *93*

veterinarians, 39
Volunteer sign-up, *20, 21*, 22, 45, *58*

Wagner Creek floods,
Wagner Creek pumping stations, 43
Wagner Creek, floods, 38, 44-45; *128, 129;* wrecks houses, 44-45
Wal-Mart parking lot, *90*

Water Street collapse, *14*, 22, 43, 45, *71;* (map), *13*
water, delivery of, *35*
water, swim pool as source, *35*
water, theft of, 31
Webber, Bert, vi, 13, 18, *141*
Webber, Margie, 18, *141*
Webber, Michael E. (photog), 40
Websters Handspinners (etc.), *iii, 44*
Wendy's (hamburgers), 31
Westerfield, Virginia, experiences, 29-30
Winburn Way, *11, 14,* 15, 31, *33*, 45; (map), *12, 13*
Winburn Way, inundated, 23
World's Largest Coffee Cup," 76, *141*

Zundel, Dr. Rob't., experiences, 26-29, Luman Road (flooded), *27*
"Zundel Lake," *27, 28*